Y0-EIA-423

Oxford Crest

MARKETING TOOLS

TOOLS

— for —

BUSINESS
EXECUTIVES

MARKETING
TOOLS
— *for* —
BUSINESS
EXECUTIVES

John L. Fortenberry, Jr.

Oxford Crest

OXFORD, MISSISSIPPI

Oxford Crest, Inc.
Post Office Box 334
Oxford, Mississippi 38655

www.OxfordCrest.com

Printed in the United States of America.

Library of Congress Cataloging-in-Publication Data

Fortenberry, John L.
  Marketing tools for business executives / John L. Fortenberry, Jr.
      p. cm.
Includes bibliographical references.
  ISBN 0-9717418-1-6 (cloth : alk. paper)
 1. Marketing—Management. I. Title.
  HF5415.13.F625 2004
  658.8—dc22
                                          2004002989

Dedicated to My Mother

Mary Margaret Mosal Fortenberry

Contents

Part Three
CONSUMER BEHAVIOR & PRODUCT PROMOTIONS TOOLS

Part Four
ENVIRONMENTAL ANALYSIS & COMPETITIVE ASSESSMENT TOOLS

Part Five
MARKETING STRATEGY & PLANNING TOOLS

PREFACE

Modern organizations compete in what might be considered the most competitive marketplace of all time in an environment of immense and ever-increasing complexity. On an ongoing basis, establishments of all kinds—banks, airlines, automobile manufacturers, technology firms, hospitals, hotels, restaurants, and so on—vie against one another in their respective markets for the opportunity to serve customers. Each of these organizations ultimately is in search of growth and prosperity, and the best managed of these entities will indeed realize this goal.

Marketing is possibly the most critical management responsibility associated with the pursuit and realization of growth and prosperity. Marketing can broadly be defined as *a management process that involves the assessment of customer wants and needs, and the performance of all activities associated with the development, pricing, provision, and promotion of product solutions that satisfy those wants and needs.*

Although most often associated with advertising and sales, marketing is much more encompassing as its definition implies. Aside from promotions activities, marketing includes such critical functions as environmental scanning, wants and needs assessment, new product development, target marketing, product pricing, product distribution, and market research.

Given the critical role of marketing, business executives must dedicate considerable resources, both temporal and financial, to marketing endeavors.

Aside from merely assigning resources to marketing activities, however, business executives should ideally seek their own personal understanding of marketing. To assist business executives in achieving this understanding, I authored *Marketing Tools for Business Executives.*

Written for business executives from the perspective of the marketing professional, *Marketing Tools for Business Executives* presents a series of thirty essential marketing tools and demonstrates their application in the business environment.

The tools presented in this work cover a fairly broad spectrum of marketing including product development and portfolio analysis, target marketing, consumer behavior and product promotions, environmental analysis and competitive assessment, and marketing strategy and planning. The specific tools selected from these broad categories range from time-tested marketing management classics to new models that will undoubtedly become classics in time.

Each chapter of this work focuses on a specific marketing tool and, if desired, can be read as a stand-alone document—a convenience that greatly increases the utility of *Marketing Tools for Business Executives*.

For those who are new to marketing or possibly in need of refreshing their understanding of the discipline, a brief introduction is offered in the appendix of this book. A glossary of marketing terminology is also included at the conclusion of this work.

It is my hope that you will find the marketing tools presented in this book useful in your daily marketing endeavors.

John L. Fortenberry, Jr.

Acknowledgments

A special note of thanks is extended to the following individuals for their helpful comments and suggestions regarding *Marketing Tools for Business Executives*. Their assistance yielded very useful insights.

Dr. Mark Burns
Associate Professor of Political Science
Department of Political Science
Auburn University
Auburn, Alabama

Dr. Troy A. Festervand
Associate Dean for Graduate and Executive Education
and Professor of Marketing
Jennings A. Jones College of Business
Middle Tennessee State University
Murfreesboro, Tennessee

Dr. Anne Permaloff
Professor of Political Science and Public Administration
Department of Political Science and Public Administration
Auburn University at Montgomery
Montgomery, Alabama

PART ONE

PRODUCT DEVELOPMENT
&
PORTFOLIO ANALYSIS TOOLS

THE PRODUCT LIFE CYCLE

As with all living things, products have finite life spans. This is particularly evident in modern society where continuous innovation and change have become commonplace. Regardless of the particular industry examined—banking and finance, retailing, transportation, technology, healthcare, food service, and so on—innovation is pervasive.

Rapid innovation, while beneficial to society, drives existing products into obsolescence very quickly, creating obvious challenges (logistical, financial, and otherwise) for marketers who are dually charged with managing current product offerings while actively seeking to develop new products that will succeed those entering decline.

Not only do products possess limited life spans, but like their living counterparts, their life spans consist of a number of developmental stages, with each of these stages presenting its own unique array of opportunities and constraints. Products must be managed differently during the different stages of their life cycles, making it imperative for marketing managers to understand these stages and the appropriate strategies to be employed—a task facilitated by a model known as the Product Life Cycle.

Illustrated in Figure 1-1, the Product Life Cycle consists of a vertical axis representing sales, a horizontal axis representing time, a curve illustrating sales growth in relation to time, and four stages of development: intro-

FIGURE 1-1: The Product Life Cycle

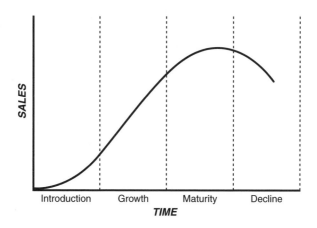

duction, growth, maturity, and decline. These stages of development are defined as follows:

Stage 1: Introduction

The introductory stage of the Product Life Cycle involves the initial presentation of a product in the market. During this stage, sales growth slowly begins to increase as the public begins to gain awareness of newly introduced product offerings through promotional efforts. Competitors are few or nonexistent at this point. Here, marketers are primarily concerned with developing innovative promotional strategies that will increase *product* awareness in the market.

Stage 2: Growth

The growth stage of the Product Life Cycle is characterized by rapidly escalating sales, courtesy of increased product awareness. This rapid sales growth generates large amounts of cash, but it also attracts competitors to the market. This necessitates that organizations reinvest the resulting cash windfalls back into these products to fend off new entrants. During this stage, marketers shift their attention from building *product* awareness to building *brand* awareness.

Stage 3: Maturity

During the maturity stage of the Product Life Cycle, sales growth levels off in what has now become an established market. Plateauing sales growth causes weaker competitors to exit the market, leaving their stronger counterparts who intensely compete for market dominance. At this point, products are the most lucrative for their organizations. Because mature offerings are established in the market, it is not necessary to reinvest the entirety of cash that these products generate. Here,

FIGURE 1-2: Product Life Cycle Variants

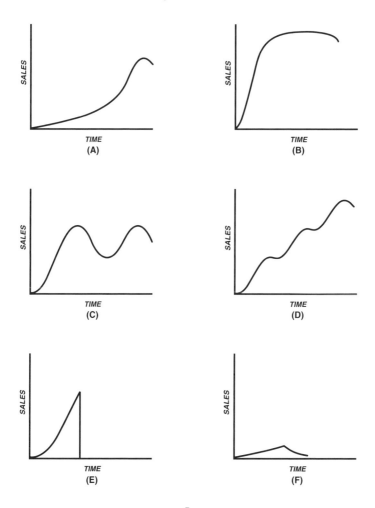

marketers seek to increase market share by further differentiating their products from competitive offerings.

Stage 4: Decline

During the decline stage of the Product Life Cycle, sales growth rapidly decreases, as well as the number of competitors in the marketplace. Falling consumer demand leads marketers to either eliminate these products or seek to extend the life spans of declining offerings through the discovery of new product uses or through product repositioning.

Product Life Cycle Variants

Although typically illustrated as an S-shaped curve, the appearance of the Product Life Cycle varies based on the marketplace experiences of product offerings. Figure 1-2 illustrates six curves that could potentially develop.

Figure 1-2A illustrates the life cycle of a product that witnessed a very lengthy ascent to maturity, possibly because the public was not ready or willing to quickly accept the new offering or perhaps because the entity had difficulties informing the public of the new product's existence. Newly established entities seeking to enter established markets with established competitors would likely face this type of life cycle scenario as they strive to develop a customer base.

Figure 1-2B depicts the life cycle of a product that gained immediate acceptance followed by a period of enduring maturity. Such a curve would possibly develop upon the discovery of a product (e.g., a breakthrough pharmaceutical, a faster microprocessor, a more fuel-efficient automobile) that was immediately welcomed by customers and successfully filled their wants and needs over the long run.

Figure 1-2C depicts the life cycle of a product that entered maturity, declined, re-entered maturity, and re-entered decline. This cyclical pattern would be representative of a product that experienced consumer interest and disinterest over time (e.g., a clothing style, a diet plan).

Figure 1-2D illustrates the life cycle of a product that re-entered the growth stage multiple times after reaching maturity. Such a curve would be representative of a product that was found to be useful for purposes beyond its original scope (e.g., baking soda, nylon, certain pharmaceuticals), resulting in extended growth beyond its initial maturity stage.

Figure 1-2E illustrates the life cycle of a product that experienced a period of rapid growth followed by an immediate decline. This type of curve would be representative of, for example, a product that was suddenly pulled from the market due to newly discovered health or safety concerns—a defective toy, a flawed automobile tire, a potentially fatal drug, and so on.

Figure 1-2F illustrates the life cycle of a product that failed after its introduction in the market. This unfortunate life cycle could possibly represent any of the multiple new product offerings that are introduced in the market but fail to achieve commercial success.

These examples illustrate only a few of the many Product Life Cycle variants that could possibly develop. Obviously, there are no guarantees that products will move through any or all of the stages of development. Given the unpredictable nature of product and market dynamics, it stands to reason that Product Life Cycles cannot be predetermined.

In Practice

Given that all products have limited lives, marketers must actively assemble and manage product portfolios that are formulated to achieve long-term growth and prosperity. The Product Life Cycle assists marketers in this endeavor, serving as a useful portfolio planning tool.

Ideally, firms will have products at all stages of the Product Life Cycle. Established offerings provide excess amounts of cash that can be used to develop and grow new products that will ensure the future viability of organizations. By assembling balanced product portfolios, marketers position their establishments for consistent, enduring growth.

In addition to its strength as a portfolio planning tool, the Product Life Cycle also serves as a guide for designing marketing strategies. Since different developmental stages require different marketing actions, the Product Life Cycle provides marketers with a decision-making tool for formulating marketing strategy.

The Product Life Cycle can also be used, as Theodore Levitt suggested in his classic 1965 article entitled "Exploit the Product Life Cycle," as a forecasting tool where marketers attempt to predict the Product Life Cycles of new or anticipated product offerings. Even though Product Life Cycles cannot be predetermined, marketing strategy can be improved by formulating potential life cycle scenarios.

In Summary

The Product Life Cycle provides marketers with an effective tool for portfolio planning, strategy formulation, and forecasting. It serves as a reminder of the limited life spans possessed by products and, hence, the necessity for product succession planning—an essential marketing task in the increasingly innovation-rich marketplace. The insights offered by the Product Life Cycle can greatly improve the marketing performance of organizations.

REFERENCE:

Levitt, Theodore. "Exploit the Product Life Cycle." *Harvard Business Review* (November/ December) 1965: 81-94.

The Booz, Allen, & Hamilton New Product Process

Given that all products possess limited life spans, a fact that is especially evident in today's ever-changing marketplace, organizations must continually seek to develop new product offerings that will ensure long-term growth and prosperity. These new products, of course, do not automatically appear in the marketplace. Instead, new products result from enormously labor intensive and expensive efforts that eventually lead to market entry.

Market entry for new offerings is further complicated by the immense rules and regulations governing many goods and services, and even if market entry is attained, there are no guarantees of commercial success, as indicated by the high incidence of new product failure.

In addition to the effort, expense, and bureaucracy associated with new product development, business establishments face yet another concern. Every time new products are presented in the market, organizations place their reputations in jeopardy. New products that are poorly developed can be quite damaging to existing offerings, presenting yet another potential disaster and an incentive for companies to work diligently to ensure new product success.

Minimizing Risk

Although risk is inherent in new product development, it can be lessened by adopting a systematic framework for managing new product activities, such as the one

FIGURE 2-1: The Booz, Allen, & Hamilton New Product Process

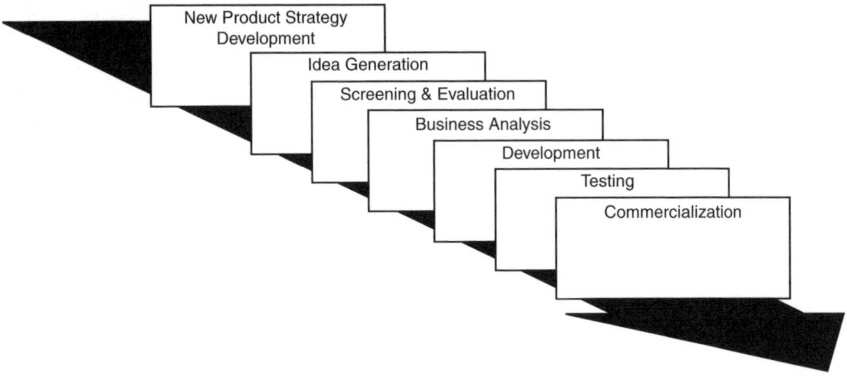

From *New Products Management for the 1980s* by Booz, Allen, & Hamilton. Copyright © 1982 by Booz, Allen, & Hamilton. Reprinted by permission of Booz, Allen, & Hamilton.

presented by the management consulting firm of Booz, Allen, & Hamilton. Illustrated in Figure 2-1, the Booz, Allen, & Hamilton New Product Process divides new product development into seven sequential stages, namely new product strategy development, idea generation, screening and evaluation, business analysis, development, testing, and commercialization. These stages are explained as follows:

Stage 1: New Product Strategy Development

The Booz, Allen, & Hamilton New Product Process begins with the development of new product strategies. Here, marketers lay the foundation for the new product process by reviewing corporate objectives and identifying roles that new products might play in satisfying these objectives. This information clarifies the strategic business requirements for new products and provides a point of reference for subsequent stages.

Stage 2: Idea Generation

During the idea generation stage, entities search for product ideas that are compatible with the goals and objectives determined in the preceding stage. The idea generation stage usually begins by conducting a self-assessment to determine the product categories that are of primary interest to given entities. Once areas of interest have been determined, organizations scan the environment in search of growth opportunities that can be exploited. Ideas should actively be solicited from any potential idea source, including employees, customers, and vendors. The ultimate purpose of the idea generation stage is to produce a wealth of ideas. Here, every idea should be welcomed and initially considered on a "can do" basis.

Stage 3: Screening & Evaluation

The screening and evaluation stage involves the analysis of all of the ideas gathered during the idea generation stage to determine which discoveries should be further investigated. Here, each idea should be envisioned as a product in the market, where it can be evaluated on its potential contribution to given entities. Through screening and evaluation, organizations seek to narrow down the number of ideas generated during the preceding stage by focusing only on those that offer the greatest potential.

During this stage, new product ideas decrease; however, the expenses associated with new product development increase—a trend that continues through the remaining stages of the new product process, as indicated in Figures 2-2 and 2-3, respectively. Organizations can only afford to develop those ideas that possess the greatest potential for success in the market. The most promising ideas move to the business analysis stage and all others are eliminated.

Stage 4: Business Analysis

During the business analysis stage, the most promising product ideas are subjected to intense scrutiny to determine their potential for translation into commercially successful offerings. Here, hypothetical business plans are formulated for these offerings which identify product attributes, barriers to entry, current and potential competitors, target markets, market growth information, financial projections, promotional methods, and so on in an effort to formulate preliminary business recommendations. Successful product ideas graduate to the development stage.

Stage 5: Development

During the development stage, product ideas that have successfully met the scrutiny forwarded during prior stages are translated into actual product offerings. For goods, development involves the actual physical assembly of the offerings. For services, development involves the assembly of all components required for the services to be offered, such as office space, equipment, operating permits, and personnel.

During this stage, product offerings may go through many alterations—a usual occurrence when on-paper ideas are translated into real world offerings. Alterations continue through the remaining stages of the new product process as goods and services are readied for the market.

FIGURE 2-2: Mortality of New Product Ideas

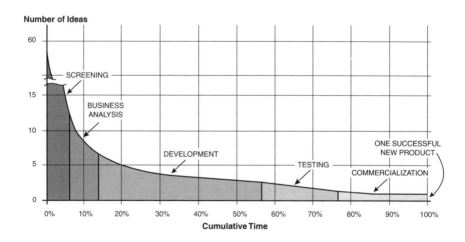

From *Management of New Products* by Booz, Allen, & Hamilton. Copyright © 1968 by Booz, Allen, & Hamilton. Reprinted by permission of Booz, Allen, & Hamilton.

Stage 6: Testing

Testing seeks to validate earlier business projections associated with new offerings through commercial experimentation. Here, new products are readied for commercialization by conducting trials to determine marketplace suitability, with the nature of the testing being dependent on the characteristics of the particular products under development and the markets sought.

Because of their tangibility, goods are particularly well suited for laboratory testing, as well as test marketing—a practice where marketers directly or indirectly seek consumer feedback regarding their new products. Bedding manufacturers, for example, subject their products to intensive laboratory testing to ensure that their offerings meet designated quality standards. These companies might also test market their products by providing individuals with pillows, mattresses, or other items in exchange for their comments regarding the utility and comfort of the particular product offerings.

FIGURE 2-3: Cumulative New Product Expenditures

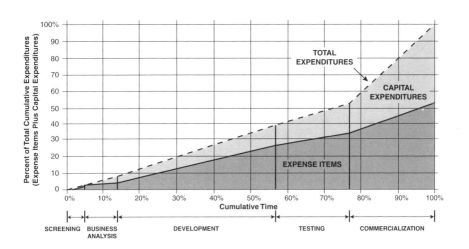

From *Management of New Products* by Booz, Allen, & Hamilton. Copyright © 1968 by Booz, Allen, & Hamilton. Reprinted by permission of Booz, Allen, & Hamilton.

Beverage companies, too, actively engage in laboratory testing as they endeavor to perfect existing products or develop entirely new items for distribution. These companies are also actively engaged in test marketing. They might, for example, test market a newly developed soft drink in several major cities to assess consumer demand, making adjustments as needed prior to the product's national introduction.

Like their tangible counterparts, services can also be tested and test marketed, albeit in a different manner. Certainly, prior to its grand opening, a bank would undergo an intensive battery of tests to ensure

TABLE 2-1: Causes of New Product Failure

1. **Market/marketing failure**
   Small size of the potential market
   No clear product differentiation
   Poor positioning
   Misunderstanding of customer needs
   Lack of channel support
   Competitive response

2. **Financial failure**
   Low return on investment

3. **Timing failure**
   Late in the market
   "Too" early—market not yet developed

4. **Technical failure**
   Product did not work
   Bad design

5. **Organizational failure**
   Poor fit with the organizational culture
   Lack of organizational support

6. **Environmental failure**
   Government regulations
   Macro-economic factors

From "Managing New Product Development for Strategic Competitive Advantage" by Dipak Jain in *Kellogg on Marketing*, edited by Dawn Iacobucci. Copyright © 2001 by John Wiley & Sons, Inc. Reprinted by permission of John Wiley & Sons, Inc.

that equipment is working properly, that necessary resources are available, that employees understand their duties and responsibilities, etc. The bank might even decide to test market its services by assembling a group of consumers to receive service offerings and provide feedback. The bank might, for example, offer savings bonds or free checking accounts to individuals in exchange for their comments and opinions regarding the bank's accessibility, decor, customer service, and so on.

The feedback generated through testing provides marketers with yet another opportunity to ready their products for entry in the marketplace. Once any necessary alterations are made, products are ready for commercialization.

Stage 7: Commercialization

Commercialization involves the full-scale market introduction of newly developed products. As new products enter the market, ongoing customer feedback should actively be sought to ensure that products meet and, ideally, exceed customer expectations. Any new product "bugs" that are identified should quickly be remedied. Aside from ensuring a trouble-free marketplace introduction, marketers must carefully monitor competitor reactions to their new product offerings, taking steps when necessary to counteract competitive responses.

Risk & Failure

Risk is an inherent part of new product development where new product failures routinely outnumber successes. These failures are caused by a variety of factors, as illustrated in Table 2-1. New product failures are prevalent across all industries, serving to greatly increase the costs of new product development and, hence, the associated risks.

Despite these risks, however, entities must engage in the new product process if they wish to endure and prosper. Only through the adoption of a systematic framework for managing new product activities can marketers minimize associated risks and increase their chances of developing new goods and services that achieve commercial success.

In Summary

The Booz, Allen, & Hamilton New Product Process serves as a useful guide for new product development. Its seven sequential stages (new product strategy development, idea generation, screening and evaluation, business analysis, development, testing, and commercialization) provide invaluable guidance to marketers seeking to develop new products in a comprehensive and orderly fashion.

REFERENCES:

Booz, Allen, & Hamilton. *Management of New Products*. New York: Booz, Allen, & Hamilton, 1968.

Booz, Allen, & Hamilton. *New Products Management for the 1980s*. New York: Booz, Allen, & Hamilton, 1982.

Jain, Dipak. "Managing New Product Development for Strategic Competitive Advantage." In *Kellogg on Marketing*, edited by Dawn Iacobucci. New York: Wiley, 2001.

Theodore Levitt's Total Product Concept

Products are much more than one-dimensional items. Instead, they represent complex bundles of attributes that are purchased and consumed by customers to satisfy wants and needs. The success of goods and services in the marketplace is largely based on the skillful assembly of associated product attributes in a manner that will attract and retain customers. Therefore, marketers must possess a thorough understanding of the multidimensional nature of products.

The Total Product Concept, which was formulated by Theodore Levitt, illustrates the multidimensional nature of products and provides guidance to marketers seeking to develop goods and services that meet and exceed the expectations of customers. Presented in Figure 3-1, Levitt's Total Product Concept involves four product levels (generic, expected, augmented, and potential) that are depicted by four concentric circles.

As products move from inner levels to outer levels, they become increasingly complex and offer marketers enhanced opportunities to differentiate goods and services from competitive offerings. The four product levels are defined as follows:

The Generic Product

The generic product, which could also be referred to as the core product, is an offering in its most basic and rudimentary form. At this level, competitive products are virtually indistinguishable from one another as they represent only core offerings and nothing more. Customers expect more than base offerings.

The Expected Product

The expected product consists of the generic product along with features that allow it to be distinguished from competitive offerings. Expected products add branding, product features, product quality, packaging, and like elements to generic products to create offerings that can easily be recognized by customers. At this level, goods and services meet the minimum expectations of customers. In essence, these offerings represent what customers *expect* to receive.

FIGURE 3-1: Levitt's Total Product Concept

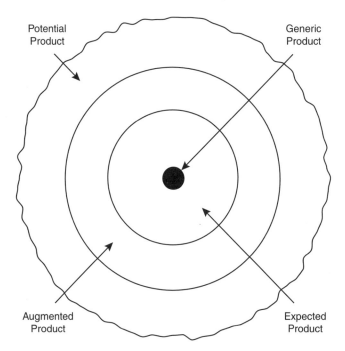

Potential
Product

Generic
Product

Augmented
Product

Expected
Product

The Augmented Product

The augmented product consists of the expected product plus additional features that extend beyond the expectations of customers. Product augmentations vary based on the nature of given offerings but typical examples include personalized service, product enhancements, warranties and guarantees, and extended service plans. Augmentations allow marketers to further differentiate their products from competitive offerings. The differentiation offered by specific augmentations may decline over time as consumers become accustomed to the enhancements and come to expect these additions, necessitating that marketers discover new ways to augment their products.

The Potential Product

The potential product represents all things that can potentially be incorporated into offerings to attract and retain customers. Whereas augmented products represent everything that is *currently* being done to attract and retain customers, potential products represent everything that *might* be done. As current augmentations become expected by customers, marketers must formulate future methods to augment, and thus differentiate, their products. The potential product level identifies these future augmentations.

In Practice

To assess products using Levitt's Total Product Concept, marketers simply (1) identify the product to be evaluated, (2) construct the Total Product Concept diagram as illustrated in Figure 3-1, (3) identify and/or formulate the generic, expected, augmented, and potential components for the product under evaluation, and (4) place the identified components on the diagram accordingly. The resulting Total Product Concept diagram is then analyzed to gain product insights.

Figure 3-2 identifies an example of Levitt's Total Product Concept applied to a vehicle offered by an automobile manufacturer. The core offering provided by the automobile is personal transportation. This generic offering is transformed into an expected product through a variety of additions including excellent dealer service, proven safety and reliability, and an industry-standard warranty. The manufacturer has further differentiated its automobile from competitive offerings through augmentations such as a leather interior, a multi-disc CD changer, high performance, and free routine maintenance. Future differentiation could occur through enhanced performance, better fuel efficiency, an extended warranty, and so on.

FIGURE 3-2: An Automobile Company's Total Product Concept

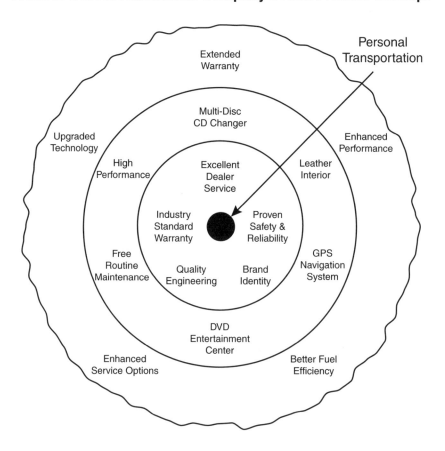

Figure 3-3 identifies an example of Levitt's Total Product Concept applied to an apartment building. The facility's generic product consists of the residential living accommodations that it offers to tenants. This base offering is transformed into the expected product through various features including free parking, reasonable lease terms, clean living quarters, and friendly staff members. Augmentations include free internet access, multiple swimming pools, round-the-clock security, and so on. Future differentiation opportunities include enhanced

---

FIGURE 3-3: An Apartment Building's Total Product Concept

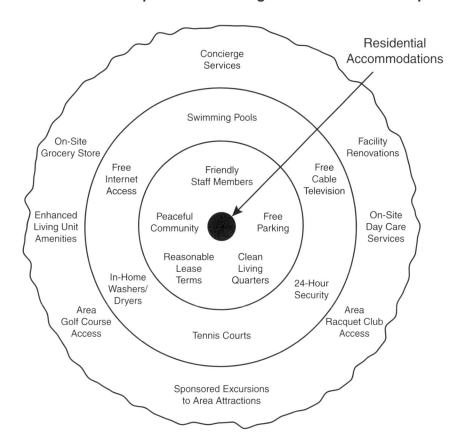

amenities in living units, facility renovations, concierge services, an on-site grocery store, area golf course access, and sponsored excursions to area attractions.

Clearly, Levitt's Total Product Concept reminds marketers that products represent complex bundles of attributes that must skillfully be assembled in order to satisfy customers. It also serves as an excellent product planning and analysis tool for the level-by-level dissection of current (and even proposed) products. Through this dissection, marketers can identify and, if necessary, enhance those attributes that differentiate products from competitive offerings. They also can formulate strategies for the future differentiation of goods and services. These points of differentiation are especially useful in the development of effective promotional campaigns.

In Summary

Levitt's Total Product Concept clearly illustrates the multidimensional nature of products. By understanding the product levels identified in the Total Product Concept, marketers are better prepared to assemble the multiple attributes of goods and services in a manner that will attract and retain customers.

REFERENCES:

Levitt, Theodore. "Marketing Success Through Differentiation—of Anything." *Harvard Business Review* (January-February) 1980: 83-91.

Levitt, Theodore. *The Marketing Imagination.* New, expanded ed. New York: The Free Press, 1986.

The Calder & Reagan Brand Design Model

4

Brands are names, logos, slogans, and other references that identify goods and services, thus allowing customers to distinguish products from competitive offerings. In essence, brands give products *identity*, a component that is absolutely essential for the purposes of product differentiation. Brands can be used to identify individual products, product lines, or entire organizations and they benefit both producers and consumers, as presented in Figure 4-1. These benefits illustrate the critical importance of brands, making the successful establishment of brand identity one of the most essential tasks of marketing management.

Despite the importance of branding, the process of brand development is often conducted in an unsystematic, haphazard fashion, typically as a derivative of either the marketing plan or ad development. In an effort to bring order to this process and improve brand results, Bobby Calder and Steven Reagan formulated an approach to branding known as Brand Design and developed the Brand Design Schematic or Model to guide marketers in this approach.

Illustrated in Figure 4-2, the Brand Design Model consists of an inner circle representing the meaningful relevant value of a product and an outer circle representing verbal and visual brand expressions. The Brand Design process challenges marketers to first identify product-related meaning (meaningful relevant value) and then formulate methods to convey this meaning to customers through an arrangement of verbal and visual

FIGURE 4-1: Functions of a Brand

elements (brand expressions). Meaningful relevant value and brand expression components of this model are explained as follows:

Meaningful Relevant Value

Through branding, marketers seek to make products more meaningful to customers and one of the best methods for accomplishing this entails viewing products from the perspective of target markets. To view products through the eyes of customers, marketers must ask themselves how their products positively impact the lives of customers. When viewing products in this manner, marketers focus their attention on the prime motivator of consumer purchase activity—the ability of products to satisfy wants and needs. These inquiries ultimately yield consumer stories that are meaningful to target markets. Once consumer stories have been formulated, marketers then focus on conveyance of these stories to target markets through the formulation of brand expressions.

Brand Expressions

Brands can be expressed using verbal and visual methods. Verbal brand expressions include naming (the assignment of names to products), wording (the development of specialized vocabularies to describe product attributes—catch phrases, slogans, etc.), and describing (the scripting of phrases and sentences that elaborate upon the attributes of products—product uses, safety information, durability information, customer testimonials, etc.).

Visual brand expressions include picturing (the presentation of products using still photography and other static, illustrative methods),

---

FIGURE 4-2: The Calder & Reagan Brand Design Model

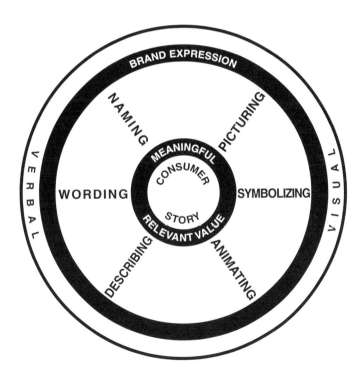

From "Brand Design" by Bobby J. Calder and Steven J. Reagan in *Kellogg on Marketing*, edited by Dawn Iacobucci. Copyright © 2001 by John Wiley & Sons, Inc. Reprinted by permission of John Wiley & Sons, Inc.

symbolizing (the development and use of logos and other abstract, symbolic methods to identify products), and animating (the use of "moving pictures" including video photography and computer animation to present products). During the brand expression stage of the Brand Design process, the ultimate goal is to develop verbal and visual components that will accurately convey the meaning of products (the consumer stories identified in the meaningful relevant value stage) to target markets.

In Practice

To develop brands using the Calder and Reagan Brand Design approach, marketers simply (1) identify the product to be branded, (2) construct the Brand Design diagram as illustrated in Figure 4-2, (3) identify and/or formulate a product-related story that is of interest to target markets, along with verbal and visual brand expressions that will convey this story to customers, and (4) place these elements on the Brand Design diagram accordingly. The resulting diagram yields a customer-focused brand identity for the given product offering.

Figure 4-3 illustrates a Brand Design Model for a newly established tire company. Here, the company has identified a relevant story of consumer interest (the peace of mind associated with safe automobile transportation courtesy of high-quality, dependable tires) and has designed its verbal and visual expressions around this story.

Quite clearly, each verbal and visual element directly relates to the safety and security afforded to drivers who purchase the company's tires. Courtesy of the Brand Design Model, the tire company has successfully formulated a customer-focused brand identity that will allow it to effectively market tires to its target audience. Coordinated promotional efforts can now be initiated.

The tire company's completed schematic clearly illustrates the power of the Brand Design approach. In one simple diagram, marketers can view the strategic and tactical brand fundamentals associated with given product offerings. This centralized source of carefully prepared

FIGURE 4-3: A Tire Company's Brand Design Model

information is particularly useful in achieving consistency of presentation across advertising media. Given the increasing array of available media, along with desires for more precise target marketing, the Brand Design Model offers marketers a method for ensuring integrated marketing communications.

It should be noted that the Brand Design process is to be conducted in an inclusive fashion where input from all organizational members involved in the development and management of associated goods and services is actively encouraged. The multiple perspectives offered by this extended group of individuals can greatly enhance resulting Brand Designs.

In Summary

Brands allow customers to distinguish goods and services from competitive offerings and are, therefore, essential for the purposes of product differentiation. Given the importance of brands, marketers can substantially benefit from the systematic branding process offered by the Calder and Reagan Brand Design approach.

The Brand Design approach usefully guides marketers through the process of formulating brands that convey customer-focused meaning—an absolute requirement for attracting the patronage of target markets. Despite its simplicity, the Brand Design approach significantly improves branding results. Progressive marketers will undoubtedly find it to be an invaluable resource that greatly improves marketing efforts.

REFERENCES:

Berthon, Pierre, James M. Hulbert, and Leyland F. Pitt. "Brand Management Prognostications." *MIT Sloan Management Review* 40, no. 2 (Winter 1999): 53-65.

Calder, Bobby J., and Steven J. Reagan. "Brand Design." In *Kellogg on Marketing*, edited by Dawn Iacobucci. New York: Wiley, 2001.

THE LEDERER & HILL
BRAND PORTFOLIO MOLECULE

5

Brands are names, logos, slogans, and other identifiers that are developed and assigned to products to help customers distinguish goods and services from competitive offerings. By successfully branding products, marketers greatly increase the likelihood that customers will recognize their goods and services—an essential prerequisite for purchase activity.

Given the obvious importance of branding, marketers must diligently work to ensure that they thoroughly understand the brands they are responsible for managing. The better marketers understand brands, the better prepared they will be to appropriately manage these offerings.

One of the most effective tools for understanding brands is known as the Brand Portfolio Molecule which, as illustrated in Figure 5-1, presents brand portfolios in the form of atoms. Developed by Chris Lederer and Sam Hill, the Brand Portfolio Molecule multidimensionally illustrates the relationships that exist among brands within given product portfolios. The Brand Portfolio Molecule also identifies, in the same multidimensional fashion, associated external brands that impact these portfolios.

Components of the Brand Portfolio Molecule

A Brand Portfolio Molecule consists of a large central atom (the lead brand) which represents the most influential brand within a given portfolio; mid-sized atoms (strategic brands) which heavily influence customer purchases; and small atoms (support brands) which mildly influence customer purchases.

The color of atoms in the Brand Portfolio Molecule indicates the influence that particular brands have within the portfolio. A light color indicates a positive influence, a medium color indicates a neutral influence, and a dark color indicates a negative influence.

Nodes are atoms (brands) that have relationships with other atoms (brands), with direct connections indicating direct relationships and indirect connections indicating indirect relationships. The width of the link between nodes indicates the degree of control that one brand commands over the other. Thicker links indicate greater control.

FIGURE 5-1: A Shipping Company's Brand Portfolio Molecule

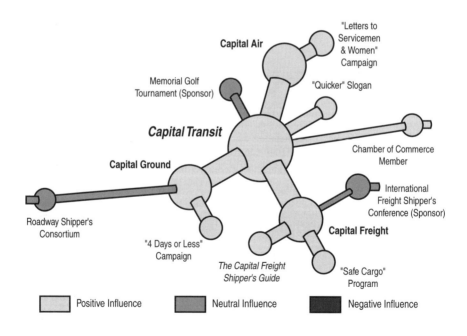

Constructed using design methodology in "See Your Brands Through Your Customers' Eyes" by Chris Lederer and Sam Hill. *Harvard Business Review* (June) 2001: 125-133.

Proximity indicates the positioning characteristics of brands. Brands that are close in proximity are similarly positioned. Brands that are more distant in proximity are more distinctly positioned.

In Practice

Marketers wishing to assemble a Brand Portfolio Molecule simply (1) list all of the brands within a given portfolio, as well as associated external brands, (2) classify each brand as lead, strategic, or support, (3) establish the network of relationships that exist among these brands, and (4) map the Brand Portfolio Molecule either by hand or with the assistance of illustration software. Once mapped, marketers use the Brand Portfolio Molecule to assess given brand portfolios.

Figure 5-1 illustrates a Brand Portfolio Molecule developed for a shipping company. From the Molecule, it is easily determined that Capital Transit is the lead brand, as it is the largest atom in the diagram. Capital Transit is positively influenced by its "Quicker" slogan and its membership in the Chamber of Commerce. The company is neutrally influenced by its sponsorship of the Memorial Golf Tournament. Capital Transit serves as the umbrella brand for three distinct units that provide positive influences: Capital Air, Capital Ground, and Capital Freight.

Capital Air is positively influenced by its relationship with its parent, Capital Transit, as well as the "Letters to Servicemen and Women" campaign that it conducts. Capital Ground is positively influenced by its relationship with Capital Transit and its "4 Days or Less" campaign, and is neutrally influenced by its membership in the Roadway Shipper's Consortium. Capital Freight is positively influenced by its relationship with Capital Transit, its distribution of *The Capital Freight Shipper's Guide*, and its "Safe Cargo" program. Capital Freight is neutrally influenced by its sponsorship of the International Freight Shipper's Conference.

The Brand Portfolio Molecule clearly illustrates that Capital Transit possesses a strong array of brands, with positive influences dominating its portfolio. The company is particularly fortunate not to have any brands that negatively influence the portfolio. With this information, Capital Transit can focus its attention on maintaining the numerous positive components of its brand portfolio.

In Summary

The Lederer and Hill Brand Portfolio Molecule provides marketers with a valuable tool for understanding the relationships that exist within brand portfolios. By clearly demonstrating internal brand relationships, as well as relationships that exist with associated external brands, the Brand Portfolio Molecule allows marketers to easily identify strong, neutral, and weak points associated with their brands. With its succinct presentation of given brand portfolios and associated relationships, the Brand Portfolio Molecule clearly facilitates brand management activities.

REFERENCE:

Lederer, Chris, and Sam Hill. "See Your Brands Through Your Customers' Eyes." *Harvard Business Review* (June) 2001: 125-133.

KEVIN LANE KELLER'S BRAND REPORT CARD

Branding, the development, assignment, and management of names, logos, slogans, and other identifiers associated with products, is one of the most important activities of marketing management. Through branding, marketers give their products *identity*. This *identity* allows customers to distinguish goods and services from competitive offerings.

Branding activities do not cease with the introduction of products in the marketplace. Instead, these activities are ongoing. Consumers, their wants and needs, their preferences, their perceptions, and their environments are constantly changing. Brands and the products they represent must keep up with these changes—a task which necessitates that marketing managers devote significant attention to branding throughout the product life cycle.

Given the dynamic nature of the marketplace and its consumers, marketers must periodically assess the brand performance of their given offerings in an effort to ensure that brands are meeting strategic and tactical goals and objectives. To assist marketers in the process of brand evaluation, Kevin Lane Keller developed the Brand Report Card, a useful tool that allows marketers to evaluate their offerings based on ten characteristics possessed by excellent brands.

Illustrated in Figure 6-1, Keller's Brand Report Card requires that marketers (1) read each of the ten brand characteristics, (2) rate their brands on a scale of one

FIGURE 6-1: Keller's Brand Report Card

Rating Your Brand

Instructions: Rate your brand on a scale of one to ten (one being extremely poor and ten being extremely good) for each characteristic below. Then create a bar chart that reflects the scores. Use the bar chart to generate discussion among all those individuals who participate in the management of your brands. Looking at the results in that manner should help you identify areas that need improvement, recognize areas in which you excel, and learn more about how your particular brand is configured.

It can also be helpful to create a report card and chart for competitors' brands simply by rating those brands based on your own perceptions, both as a competitor and as a consumer. As an outsider, you may know more about how their brands are received in the marketplace than they do.

Keep that in mind as you evaluate your own brand. Try to look at it through the eyes of consumers rather than through your own knowledge of budgets, teams, and time spent on various initiatives.

 The brand excels at delivering the benefits customers truly desire.

Have you attempted to uncover unmet consumer wants and needs? By what methods? Do you focus relentlessly on maximizing your customers' product experiences? Do you have a system in place for getting comments from customers to the people who can effect change?

 The brand stays relevant.

Have you invested in product improvements that provide better value for your customers? Are you in touch with your customers' tastes? With the current market conditions? With new trends as they apply to your offering? Are your marketing decisions based on your knowledge of the above?

 The pricing strategy is based on customers' perceptions of value.

Have you optimized price, cost, and quality to meet or exceed customers' expectations? Do you have a system in place to monitor customers' perceptions of your brand's value? Have you estimated how much value your customers believe the brand adds to your product?

 The brand is properly positioned.

Have you established necessary and competitive points of parity with competitors? Have you established desirable and deliverable points of difference?

 The brand is consistent.

Are you sure that your marketing programs are not sending conflicting messages and that they haven't done so over time? Conversely, are you adjusting your programs to keep current?

FIGURE 6-1: Keller's Brand Report Card—continued

The brand portfolio and hierarchy make sense.

Can the corporate brand create a seamless umbrella for all brands in the portfolio? Do the brands in that portfolio hold individual niches? How extensively do the brands overlap? In what areas? Conversely, do the brands maximize market coverage? Do you have a brand hierarchy that is well thought out and well understood?

The brand makes use of and coordinates a full repertoire of marketing activities to build equity.

Have you chosen or designed your brand name, logo, symbol, slogan, packaging, signage, and so forth to maximize brand awareness? Have you implemented integrated marketing activities that target customers? Are you aware of all the marketing activities that involve your brand? Are the people managing each activity aware of one another? Have you capitalized on the unique capabilities of each communication option while ensuring that the meaning of the brand is consistently represented?

The brand's managers understand what the brand means to customers.

Do you know what customers like and don't like about a brand? Are you aware of all the core associations people make with your brand, whether intentionally created by your organization or not? Have you created detailed, research-driven portraits of your target customers? Have you outlined customer-driven boundaries for brand extensions and guidelines for marketing programs?

The brand is given proper support and that support is sustained over the long run.

Are the successes or failures of marketing programs fully understood before they are changed? Is the brand given sufficient R&D support? Have you avoided the temptation to cut back marketing support for the brand in reaction to a downturn in the market or a slump in sales?

The organization monitors sources of brand equity.

Have you created a brand charter that defines the meaning and equity of the brand and how it should be treated? Do you conduct periodic brand audits to assess the health of your brand and to set strategic direction? Do you conduct routine tracking studies to evaluate current market performance? Do you regularly distribute brand equity reports that summarize all relevant research and information to assist marketers in making decisions? Have you assigned explicit responsibility for monitoring and preserving brand equity?

to ten for each characteristic (with one being extremely poor and ten being extremely good), and (3) create a bar chart that reflects the results of the evaluation. This chart is then analyzed to determine strengths and weaknesses associated with brand management. The ten characteristics possessed by excellent brands are identified as follows:

Characteristic 1:
The brand excels at delivering the benefits customers truly desire.

When customers purchase products, they are buying collections of tangible and intangible attributes that satisfy wants and needs. In arranging these tangible and intangible characteristics, marketers must strive to ensure that their products incorporate the attributes that customers indeed are seeking. This, of course, first requires the identification of customer-desired features.

Identification of customer-desired attributes can be accomplished through a variety of methods. One such method is known as environmental scanning, an externally-focused activity where marketers seek to assess the environment in an effort to identify marketplace trends. Externally-focused activities are ideally supplemented by internally-focused activities. One such internally-focused activity is the customer survey which requests feedback from customers regarding their experiences, perceptions, and opinions concerning the ability of business entities to appropriately address wants and needs.

Identification of customer wants and needs is, however, only part of the equation. The other part, of course, involves the development and delivery of innovative product solutions that satisfy the identified wants and needs.

Characteristic 2:
The brand stays relevant.

Brands must stay relevant in the eyes of customers. This relevance is maintained not only by incorporating the latest new features and innovations into given offerings, but also by taking steps to ensure that the imagery associated with brands accurately reflects modern society.

Brands are image-laden. They convey feelings and emotions—aspects of human life that change over time. Given this, marketers must ensure that they devote significant attention to both the tangible and intangible aspects of branded products in an effort to keep their brands relevant in the eyes of customers.

Characteristic 3:
The pricing strategy is based on customers' perceptions of value.

Marketers must ensure that product pricing equates with the value delivered by the goods and services that are offered to customers. In essence, a balance must be struck between the price of offerings and associated product features and benefits. The more balanced the relationship, the more likely marketers can meet the value expectations of customers.

Characteristic 4:
The brand is properly positioned.

As identity vehicles, brands are essential to the practice of product positioning, where marketers seek to influence customer perceptions of their offerings by determining an appropriate and effective "image" for products to convey to targeted audiences. In positioning products, marketers must determine, for example, whether they have established appropriate *points of parity* (areas where products meet the strengths of competitive offerings) and *points of difference* (areas where products outperform competitive offerings).

An air carrier, for example, that successfully incorporates these points essentially communicates to customers that it offers all of the benefits of competing air carriers, plus added benefits (e.g., friendlier service, better connections, fewer delays, lower prices, better frequent flyer programs).

Products that are poorly positioned are destined to fail because they do not elicit desired perceptions in the minds of customers. Given this, marketers must place significant attention on this important marketing aspect.

Characteristic 5:
The brand is consistent.

One of the most important aspects of branding involves consistency in the presentation of product brands in the marketplace. Given the ever-increasing array of advertising media that marketers have at their disposal, achieving consistency in presentation has become a most challenging task.

If a hospital, for example, simultaneously portrays itself as "the leader in the altruistic delivery of patient care" in its radio and television campaigns; "the leader in the technological delivery of patient care" in its print and outdoor media campaigns; and "the leader in the economical delivery of patient care" in its internet campaign, customers will undoubtedly be confused by the conflicting messages that are being sent.

For given promotional campaigns over given periods of time, it is essential for marketers to deliver the same, consistent message to customers across all advertising media, thus alleviating the confusion associated with multiple, conflicting messages.

Characteristic 6:
The brand portfolio and hierarchy make sense.

The number of brands held by organizations varies considerably depending on the characteristics of associated business entities. Business entities that offer a limited array of products will likely need only one brand to represent both the given establishment and its product offerings. Business entities that offer a wide variety of products, however, will probably need to develop multiple brands that accurately represent their many product offerings.

When multiple brands exist, it is very important for marketers to ensure that their brand portfolios (the overall collection of brands held by an organization) and brand hierarchies (the method of organizing brands within a brand portfolio) are appropriate. Importantly, marketers must ensure that they do not place too many products under one brand name. They also must ensure that they avoid overlapping two brands within the same portfolio.

All brands impact the value of associated brand portfolios. The better organized the brands, the more likely the arrangement will make sense to marketers and their targeted audiences. Appropriately arranged hierarchies, in essence, facilitate brand performance.

Characteristic 7:
The brand makes use of and coordinates a full repertoire of marketing activities to build equity.

Every marketing effort represents an opportunity to increase brand awareness, thus increasing brand equity—the value of a brand. Marketers must be certain to make use of these opportunities by ensuring that brand names, logos, symbols, etc. are prominently featured in advertisements and other promotional campaigns in an effort to facilitate brand awareness.

Brands serve as identity vehicles for goods and services. Failure to appropriately incorporate them into associated marketing campaigns is most wasteful.

Characteristic 8:
The brand's managers understand what the brand means to customers.

Brands have meaning. Some aspects of brands may be viewed positively by customers, while other aspects may be viewed negatively. By understanding exactly what brands mean to customers, marketers are better prepared to make decisions involving product offerings. Failure to view brands through the eyes of customers can lead to disaster.

A bank, for example, that has achieved a reputation for offering timely service to patrons would likely lose a considerable portion of its customer base if it instituted a policy to double the number of transactions handled by its existing array of bank tellers. Such a move would undoubtedly create extended delays, immediately eroding the bank's now *former* brand asset of timely service.

Progressive marketers understand what brands mean to customers. With this understanding, they can make appropriate decisions that build brand equity.

Characteristic 9:
The brand is given proper support and that support is sustained over the long run.

Building and maintaining brand equity requires a significant and sustained investment. All too often, however, business entities withdraw funding after initial marketing success, believing that newly established brands have the power to maintain and possibly grow market share without additional resource expenditures. When this occurs, however, it opens the door for competitors to easily take away any market share victories gained by entities.

Whether the retrenchment of resources is in the form of reduced advertising dollars, reduced research and development expenditures, or even the declining interest of top executives, brand performance will undoubtedly suffer, dramatically increasing the likelihood of product failure. As with any administrative function, removal of support, attention, and other resources ultimately results in the decline and likely demise of the given function. Quite obviously, marketers must work to ensure that appropriate, sustained resources are devoted to brands.

Characteristic 10:
The organization monitors sources of brand equity.

Prudent brand management requires the ongoing assessment of brand performance in the marketplace. Ideally, marketers should periodically conduct a *brand equity audit* that includes a *brand inventory* (an internal compilation identifying all of the brands held by an organization along with detailed information outlining how each brand is to be marketed) and a *brand exploratory* (an external analysis that seeks to discover what brands mean to customers).

If this information is then placed in a *brand equity charter* (a formal document that identifies and describes brand management fundamentals associated with given product offerings), marketers are afforded with an invaluable tool that (1) assesses current brand performance and (2) provides guidance for brand management. Without such evaluative tools, brand equity and its associated sources cannot accurately be assessed.

In Practice

Figure 6-2 illustrates a bar chart that reflects the results of a Brand Report Card that was completed for a clothing company. This dia-

FIGURE 6-2: A Clothier's Brand Report Card Bar Chart

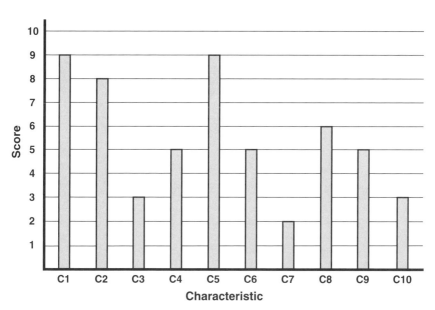

gram clearly depicts the organization's brand performance, notably indicating strengths in Characteristics 1, 2, and 5 and weaknesses in Characteristics 3, 7, and 10. With this information, marketers can take steps to build upon strengths and reduce or eliminate weaknesses, thus increasing brand performance. Any adjustments, however, should be made cautiously, making sure not to disrupt current strengths.

If desired, marketers could gain additional insights by completing Brand Report Cards for competing products, as this would likely yield useful information regarding rival offerings.

In Summary

Through its identification of ten characteristics possessed by excellent brands, Keller's Brand Report Card provides marketers with a useful tool for assessing brands. This evaluative device greatly simplifies the activity of monitoring brand performance, providing marketers with concise brand assessments that can be used to improve brand management activities, thus increasing brand equity.

REFERENCE:

Keller, Kevin Lane. "The Brand Report Card." *Harvard Business Review* (January-February) 2000: 147-157.

The Boston Consulting Group's Growth/Share Matrix

7

Successful business entities must strive to assemble balanced product portfolios that will ensure long-term growth and prosperity. Since all products have defined life spans, it is necessary to plan for the future by developing new products that will eventually succeed mature offerings.

Successful, established products generate large amounts of cash, while new, developing products rarely generate any revenue. It is with the excess cash generated by established offerings that new products emerge and gain market share in their high growth environments.

The successful assembly of a balanced product portfolio requires that marketers maintain a keen awareness of the characteristics of the products they are responsible for managing. This awareness is attained, in part, by conducting a portfolio analysis. Through such an analysis, marketers comprehensively review their product offerings in an effort to identify strengths and weaknesses, making alterations and enhancements as necessary.

To analyze product portfolios, marketers often rely on the Boston Consulting Group's Growth/Share Matrix. Illustrated in Figure 7-1, the BCG Growth/Share Matrix evaluates products based on market growth and market share characteristics.

Market growth is a measure of a market's momentum or lack thereof, while market share is a measure of an entity's portion of the total sales in a given market for a given product. The BCG Growth/Share Matrix consists of a vertical axis representing market growth (high and low), a horizontal axis representing market share (high and low), and four cells identified as cash cows, stars, question marks, and dogs. These four cells are explained as follows:

Cash Cows
(Low Growth, High Market Share)

A cash cow is a product that possesses a strong market position in a low growth market. Cash cows generate large amounts of cash, typically in excess of that required to maintain market share. Hence, cash cows are very profitable. The sizeable revenues that they generate can be used to develop other goods and services in associated portfolios.

Stars
(High Growth, High Market Share)

A star is a product that possesses a significant share of a rapidly growing market. Although stars generate large amounts of cash, the cash must be reinvested in order to maintain market share in the high growth environment. If stars maintain their market positions, they will eventually become cash cows when market growth levels off along with the associated reinvestment requirements.

Question Marks
(High Growth, Low Market Share)

A question mark is a product that has a weak market position in an environment of rapid growth. Although the market is quite attractive, the market share possessed by these product offerings is not. If question marks maintain their market positions, they will eventually become dogs. However, if market share can be increased, question marks can become stars and eventually cash cows. Increasing market share, however, requires significant investment which must come from other sources, most notably cash cows, as question marks cannot independently generate the necessary cash.

FIGURE 7-1: The BCG Growth/Share Matrix

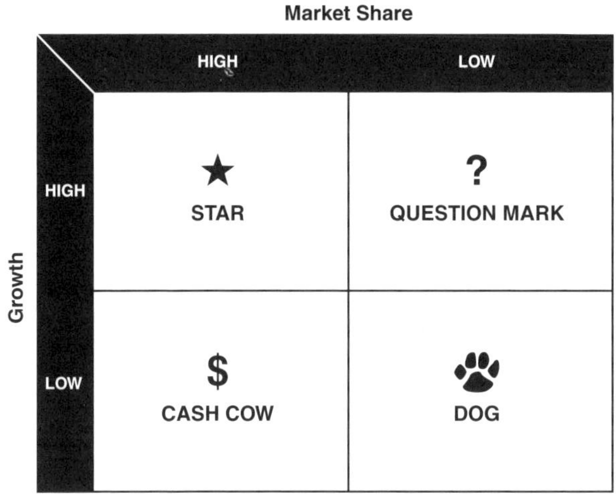

Adapted from "The Product Portfolio" (1970) by Bruce D. Henderson in *Perspectives on Strategy from the Boston Consulting Group*, edited by Carl W. Stern and George Stalk, Jr. Copyright © 1998 by The Boston Consulting Group, Inc. Reprinted by permission of John Wiley & Sons, Inc.

Dogs
(Low Growth, Low Market Share)

A dog is a product that possesses a weak market position in an environment of little growth. Dogs are generally cash drains on entities and even when they do show an accounting profit, the profit must be reinvested in order to maintain market share. Unless compensating factors exist, dogs should ideally be divested, freeing resources to be directed toward more profitable pursuits.

Market Dynamics

Since market growth eventually slows down, all products will eventually become either cash cows or dogs. This fact necessitates that marketers diligently pursue market leadership positions for all of their products during periods of growth. Leadership positions will pay dividends when growth slows and reinvestment requirements become minimal.

In Practice

To assess products using the BCG Growth/Share Matrix, marketers simply (1) identify the offerings they wish to evaluate, (2) construct the Growth/Share Matrix as illustrated in Figure 7-1, (3) gather product-related growth/share data, and (4) plot each product on the Growth/Share Matrix using circles, with larger circles representing products with larger shares of the market.

This visual representation is then analyzed to determine the strengths and weaknesses associated with given product portfolios. If additional detail is desired, marketers can forecast the market positions of products at some point in the future and plot these predictions on the Growth/Share Matrix using contrasting circles.

FIGURE 7-2: A Computer Company's Growth/Share Matrix

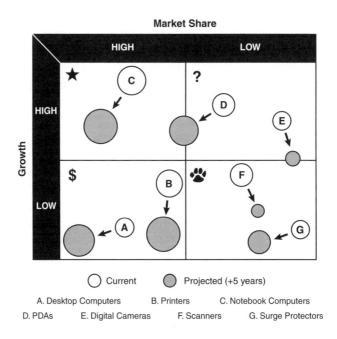

Adapted from "The Product Portfolio" (1970) by Bruce D. Henderson in *Perspectives on Strategy from the Boston Consulting Group*, edited by Carl W. Stern and George Stalk, Jr. Copyright © 1998 by The Boston Consulting Group, Inc. Reprinted by permission of John Wiley & Sons, Inc.

Figure 7-2 identifies a BCG Growth/Share Matrix (current and fore-casted) developed for a computer company. The seven white circles identify the computer company's seven product categories—desktop computers, notebook computers, printers, PDAs, digital cameras, scanners, and surge protectors. The seven shaded circles represent the market share estimates for these product categories in five years. A review of this matrix indicates that the computer company currently has two cash cows, one star, two question marks, and two dogs.

Overall, the current and forecasted portfolios of this enterprise appear very strong. The computer company is fortunate to have two cash cows generating revenues that can be used to fund other product categories. With continued investment, its star can be converted into a cash cow as its market matures. The question marks must carefully be evaluated to

FIGURE 7-3: A Bank's Growth/Share Matrix

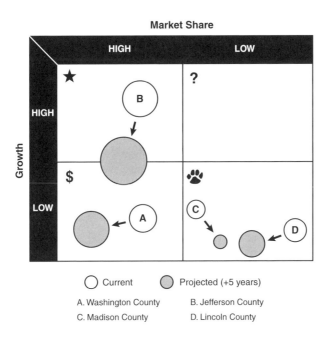

determine each category's potential contribution. If the five-year forecast is accurate, it appears that the PDA category represents a worthy investment, as it is anticipated to become a star. However, the digital camera category is expected to lose market share and drift into the dog quadrant. The digital camera category, along with the two dogs (the scanner and surge protector categories), should be divested unless compensating factors exist.

Figure 7-3 identifies a BCG Growth/Share Matrix (current and forecasted) developed for a bank with operations in four different geographic locations: Washington County, Jefferson County, Madison County, and Lincoln County. Currently, the institution possesses one cash cow, one star, no question marks, and two dogs. Washington and Jefferson markets are clearly beneficial and are expected to remain so in the future. The Madison and Lincoln markets, however, represent portfolio liabilities. Obviously, the bank would do well to exit these markets and concentrate exclusively on the prosperous Washington and Jefferson markets, unless compensating factors exist, of course.

In Summary

The Boston Consulting Group's Growth/Share Matrix provides marketers with a simple, yet highly effective, portfolio analysis tool. Notably, the Matrix assists marketers in their endeavors to assemble balanced product portfolios. Given the importance of assembling such portfolios, progressive marketers will find the Boston Consulting Group's Growth/Share Matrix to be an invaluable resource that greatly improves marketing efforts.

REFERENCE:

Henderson, Bruce D. "The Product Portfolio" (1970). In *Perspectives on Strategy from the Boston Consulting Group*, edited by Carl W. Stern and George Stalk, Jr. New York: Wiley, 1998.

The General Electric
Strategic Business-Planning Grid

8

Portfolio analysis, an activity entailing the comprehensive review of the product offerings of entities, is an essential marketing management activity. The reason for this is obvious: Marketers must thoroughly understand their products if they are to successfully manage them.

The particular portfolio analysis tool used by marketers is dependent on the specific issues at hand and the level of analytical detail desired. Some portfolio analysis tools are very basic, while others are more sophisticated. One of the more elaborate portfolio analysis tools is known as the Strategic Business-Planning Grid, an evaluative device introduced by General Electric.

Illustrated in Figure 8-1, the GE Strategic Business-Planning Grid evaluates products based on industry attractiveness (here termed *market* attractiveness which is more appropriate for industry-specific examinations) and business strength. Market attractiveness is a measure of a particular market's desirable attributes. Business strength is a measure of organization/product prowess or lack thereof in a particular market.

The GE Strategic Business-Planning Grid consists of a vertical axis representing market attractiveness (high, medium, and low), a horizontal axis representing business strength (strong, average, and weak), and nine cells divided into three zones (1, 2, and 3) differentiated by color. Zone 1 encompasses the three cells located in the upper left corner of the Grid. Products falling within

FIGURE 8-1: The GE Strategic Business-Planning Grid

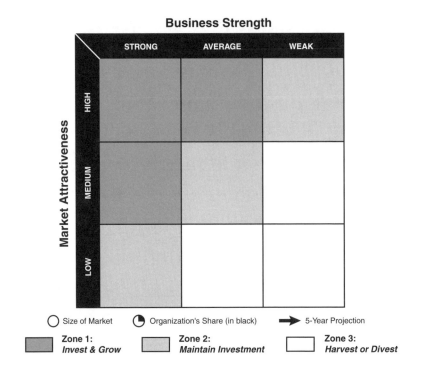

these cells represent offerings that should receive further investment for growth. Zone 2 includes the three cells running diagonally from the upper right to lower left corners of the Grid. For products falling within these cells, investment should be maintained. Zone 3 encompasses the three cells located in the lower right corner of the Grid. Products falling within these cells represent drains on portfolios and should be harvested or divested, unless compensating factors exist.

The strength of the GE Strategic Business-Planning Grid rests with the fact that its axes are designed to incorporate multiple factors associated with attractiveness and strength. This multifactor feature allows marketers to develop axes that incorporate variables that are deemed most relevant to their particular operations. The result is a customized evaluative tool.

Variables that are commonly used to compose the attractiveness axis include market size, market growth, profitability, and number of competitors. Variables that are commonly used to compose the strength axis include technological innovation, institutional capabilities, personnel, and distribution channels. The particular variables selected to compose each axis are completely up to the evaluating marketers. The only requirement is that the selected variables appropriately relate to market attractiveness and business strength.

FIGURE 8-2: A Grocery Retailer's GE Grid

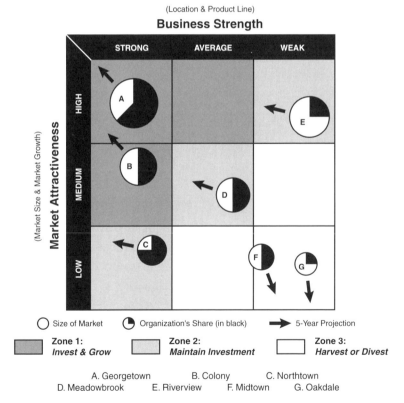

A. Georgetown   B. Colony   C. Northtown
D. Meadowbrook   E. Riverview   F. Midtown   G. Oakdale

In Practice

To assess products using the GE Strategic Business-Planning Grid, marketers simply (1) identify the product offerings they wish to evaluate, (2) construct the GE Strategic Business-Planning Grid as illustrated in Figure 8-1, (3) determine the variables that will compose the attractiveness and strength axes (weighting variables as deemed appropriate if increased detail is desired), (4) gather relevant product and market data, and (5) plot each product on the matrix using circles (which indicate market size, with larger circles indicating larger markets) and slices within each circle (which indicate the market share of given offerings).

This visual representation is then analyzed to determine the strengths and weaknesses associated with given product portfolios. If additional detail is desired, marketers can use arrows to indicate anticipated attractiveness-strength characteristics at some point in the future.

Figure 8-2 identifies a GE Strategic Business-Planning Grid (with forecast arrows) that was developed for a grocery retailer. Here, the grocery retailer evaluated its seven retail establishments (Georgetown, Colony, Northtown, Meadowbrook, Riverview, Midtown, and Oakdale) based on market attractiveness (defined by market size and market growth) and business strength (defined by store location and product line).

A review of the Grid indicates that the grocery retailer currently has two Zone 1 offerings (Georgetown and Colony), three Zone 2 offerings (Northtown, Meadowbrook, and Riverview), and two Zone 3 offerings (Midtown and Oakdale). Of the establishments identified in Zone 1, Georgetown is optimally situated with Colony closely following. Given the combination of market attractiveness and business strength characteristics, the grocery retailer would be wise to further invest in these locations in an effort to build these positions, especially given the positive five-year forecast as indicated by the diagram's arrows.

Northtown, Meadowbrook, and Riverview are situated in Zone 2. These establishments deliver neither optimal nor inferior performance;

however, the five-year forecast indicates positive attractiveness-strength characteristics. Given their placement in Zone 2, coupled with the positive forecast, the grocery retailer would be wise to maintain its level of investment in these locations.

Midtown and Oakdale are situated in Zone 3. These offerings possess inferior attractiveness-strength characteristics that are not expected to improve in the future. Unless compensating factors exist, these locations should be eliminated from the grocery retailer's portfolio.

In Summary

The General Electric Strategic Business-Planning Grid provides marketers with a useful evaluative tool that can shed significant light on the product portfolios of business entities. With its ability to incorporate multiple variables into its attractiveness and strength axes, the Grid offers marketers a truly flexible device that can be customized to address almost any scenario. Progressive marketers will undoubtedly find the General Electric Strategic Business-Planning Grid to be very useful in their endeavors to successfully manage product portfolios.

REFERENCE:

Kotler, Philip, and Gary Armstrong. *Principles of Marketing.* 8th ed. Upper Saddle River, NJ: Prentice Hall, 1999.

Igor Ansoff's
Product-Market Expansion Grid

Innovation, intense competition, and uncertainty are quite clearly staples of the modern marketplace. Given this turbulent environment, marketers must strive to proactively monitor their surroundings to, among other things, detect growth opportunities that can be exploited. No longer can marketers be satisfied with maintaining the status quo. Instead, marketers must vigorously pursue and capitalize on growth opportunities in order to increase the likelihood of institutional survival, growth, and prosperity. To capitalize on growth opportunities, marketers must carefully formulate appropriate expansion strategies—a process that is greatly facilitated by Igor Ansoff's Product-Market Expansion Grid.

Also known as Ansoff's Matrix, the Product-Market Expansion Grid was developed to shed light on the growth options available to organizations. Illustrated in Figure 9-1, the Product-Market Expansion Grid consists of a vertical axis representing markets (current and new), a horizontal axis representing products (current and new), and four cells which identify the four basic growth alternatives: market penetration, market development, product development, and diversification. These four growth strategies are defined as follows:

Market Penetration
(Current Products, Current Markets)

Market penetration is a growth strategy that seeks to increase the use of current product offerings by current customers. Here, marketing managers seek growth by identifying ways to increase consumption of the goods and services that are currently offered in existing markets. Marketing techniques used to achieve deeper market penetration include increased advertising, identification of new uses for products, price reductions, use of incentives, and so on. These techniques, when aimed at current markets, can stimulate consumption, resulting in increased growth.

Market Development
(Current Products, New Markets)

Market development is a growth strategy that involves the introduction of current products in new markets. This is achieved by identifying new target audiences and directing current offerings accordingly. Current products may, for example, be placed in different geographic markets or directed toward new demographic segments to stimulate demand and increase growth. These new markets offer new opportunities to increase the consumption of current product offerings.

FIGURE 9-1: Ansoff's Product-Market Expansion Grid

Products / Markets	Current	New
Current	*Market Penetration*	*Product Development*
New	*Market Development*	*Diversification*

Adapted from *Corporate Strategy: An Analytic Approach to Business Policy for Growth and Expansion* by H. Igor Ansoff. Copyright © 1965 by McGraw-Hill, Inc. Published by McGraw-Hill. Reprinted by permission of the Estate of H. Igor Ansoff.

Product Development
(New Products, Current Markets)

Product development is a growth strategy that involves the development and introduction of new products for use by current customers. These products might be completely different offerings or they might be modified versions of existing products. With this strategy, marketers focus their efforts on developing new goods and services that will be attractive to current customers.

Diversification
(New Products, New Markets)

Diversification is a growth strategy that involves the development and introduction of new products in new markets. By focusing on new products and new markets, this strategy calls for organizations to enter completely unfamiliar territory. Given that both aspects of this pursuit (product and market) are new to entities, diversification is the riskiest of the four growth strategies.

In Practice

To formulate growth strategies using Ansoff's Product-Market Expansion Grid, marketers simply (1) construct the Product-Market Expansion Grid as illustrated in Figure 9-1, (2) formulate growth options for each of the four growth strategies, and (3) place these growth options in their respective cells on the Grid. The resulting Product-Market Expansion Grid provides a simple, yet highly useful, depiction of available expansion opportunities.

Figure 9-2 identifies a Product-Market Expansion Grid that was developed for an airline. Here, marketers could potentially achieve deeper market penetration by increasing consumer awareness through expansion of the company's current advertising campaign. This more prominent campaign could direct more interest and attention toward the air carrier and potentially increase travel bookings. Growth could also be achieved by targeting new demographic segments and encouraging their members to select the airline for their travel needs. The airline might, for example, develop advertising campaigns that target minority and senior populations in order to attract members of these groups. Another growth option involves the introduction of gourmet in-flight meals. This new service could give the airline a competitive advantage over other carriers, improving passenger satisfaction and encouraging potential travelers to select it for their air travel needs. Finally, the airline could seek growth by diversifying into the ground transportation market by purchasing a passenger rail system.

Figure 9-3 presents a Product-Market Expansion Grid that identifies four expansion strategies for a home improvement center. The home improvement center could potentially achieve deeper market penetration by organizing several "how-to" seminars that would encourage current and potential customers to visit the establishment. These events could build awareness in the market and ultimately increase

FIGURE 9-2: An Airline's Expansion Grid

Products / Markets	Current	New
Current	**Market Penetration** — Expansion of the current advertising campaign	**Product Development** — Introduction of gourmet in-flight meals
New	**Market Development** — Direction of promotional efforts toward minority and senior citizen groups	**Diversification** — Acquisition of a passenger rail system

customer traffic. Growth could also be achieved by developing a new geographic market through the construction of a new home improvement center in a neighboring community. To improve its position in the current market, the home improvement center could introduce an installation team to serve clients who lack the ability or the desire to install products purchased from the center. Lastly, the home improvement center could seek expansion through diversification by purchasing and operating an industrial equipment dealership.

It should be noted that although each strategy in the Product-Market Expansion Grid represents a distinct path toward growth, most organizations pursue multiple growth strategies simultaneously. Importantly, the Product-Market Expansion Grid does not communicate which strategy or strategies organizations should pursue. Instead, it focuses attention on the growth opportunities that are available to entities.

FIGURE 9-3: A Home Improvement Center's Expansion Grid

Products Markets	Current	New
Current	***Market Penetration*** On-site "how-to" seminars to stimulate interest and attention	***Product Development*** Introduction of an installation team for all products sold
New	***Market Development*** Construction of a new home improvement center in a neighboring community	***Diversification*** Acquisition of an industrial equipment dealership

Adapted from *Corporate Strategy: An Analytic Approach to Business Policy for Growth and Expansion* by H. Igor Ansoff. Copyright © 1965 by McGraw-Hill, Inc. Published by McGraw-Hill. Reprinted by permission of the Estate of H. Igor Ansoff.

FIGURE 9-4: Ansoff's Expansion Cube

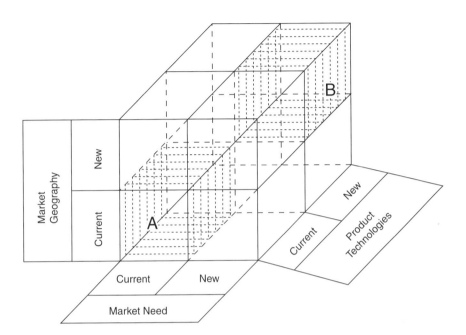

An Updated Version

It should be mentioned that Igor Ansoff developed an updated version of his Product-Market Expansion Grid, which might be termed Ansoff's Expansion Cube. Illustrated in Figure 9-4, Ansoff's Expansion Cube incorporates three dimensions, namely market need, product technologies, and market geography. These three dimensions create a cube that illustrates a variety of growth options, ranging from addressing current needs and current markets with current technologies (Section A) to addressing new needs and new markets with new technologies (Section B). Quite obviously, Ansoff's Expansion Cube offers enhanced insights into growth opportunities, making it highly useful for marketers seeking additional detail.

In Summary

The long-term viability of business entities, regardless of their industry of affiliation, largely depends on the successful identification and exploitation of growth opportunities. Igor Ansoff's Product-Market Expansion Grid provides marketers with a very powerful and effective tool for recognizing and evaluating these opportunities. This tool greatly assists marketers in the development of appropriate expansion strategies.

REFERENCES:

Ansoff, H. Igor. *Corporate Strategy: An Analytic Approach to Business Policy for Growth and Expansion.* New York: McGraw-Hill, 1965.

Ansoff, H. Igor. *The New Corporate Strategy.* Rev. ed. New York: Wiley, 1988.

PART TWO

TARGET MARKETING TOOLS

THE MARKET-PRODUCT GRID

In an effort to more effectively address the wants and needs of customers, marketers engage in target marketing, a practice that involves three interrelated activities: market segmentation, targeting, and product positioning.

Market segmentation is the process of dividing a market into groups (segments) of individuals who share common characteristics. Once the market has been segmented, marketers engage in targeting where they select (target) attractive segments and focus their efforts on satisfying the wants and needs of these groups. These targeted segments are known as an entity's target market. Product positioning follows targeting and involves the determination of an appropriate and effective "image" for products to convey to customers.

Target marketing developed out of desires to more appropriately address the various wants and needs of different customer groups. The practice stands in contrast to mass marketing which involves offering products to the market as a whole without regard for individual tastes and preferences.

Target marketing makes sense. By focusing on the specific wants and needs of market segments, marketers can deliver products that are specifically tailored for the associated groups. This practice not only improves customer satisfaction, but it also allows for better use of promotional dollars through the selection of promotions vehicles that precisely reach desired populations.

A useful tool for target marketing is known as the Market-Product Grid, which specifically addresses the segmenting and targeting aspects of target marketing.

Illustrated in Figure 10-1, the Market-Product Grid, as depicted by Eric Berkowitz, Roger Kerin, Steven Hartley, and William Rudelius, consists of a matrix with markets identified on its vertical axis and products identified on its horizontal axis. The actual number of cells in the matrix is, of course, dependent on the number of markets and products identified. As a result, Market-Product Grids range from being quite small for entities with few markets and few products to very large for entities that offer multiple markets an extensive array of products.

To create a Market-Product Grid, marketers simply (1) construct a matrix of sufficient size, (2) list potential markets on the vertical axis, (3) list product offerings on the horizontal axis, and (4) evaluate each of the resulting market-product combinations, characterizing them as large, medium, small, or nonexistent markets.

FIGURE 10-1: The Market-Product Grid

Products \ Markets	Product 1	Product 2	Product 3
Market 1	?	?	?
Market 2	?	?	?
Market 3	?	?	?

3 = Large Market, 2 = Medium Market, 1 = Small Market, 0 = No Market

TABLE 10-1: Major Segmentation Variables

GEOGRAPHIC	
World region/country	North America, Western Europe, Middle East, Pacific Rim, China, India, Canada, Mexico
Country region	Pacific, Mountain, West North Central, West South Central, East North Central, East South Central, South Atlantic, Middle Atlantic, New England
City or metro size	Under 5,000; 5,000-20,000; 20,000-50,000; 50,000-100,000; 100,000-250,000; 250,000-500,000; 500,000-1,000,000; 1,000,000-4,000,000; 4,000,000+
Density	Urban, suburban, rural
Climate	Northern, southern
DEMOGRAPHIC	
Age	Under 6, 6-11, 12-19, 20-34, 35-49, 50-64, 65+
Gender	Male, female
Family size	1-2, 3-4, 5+
Family life cycle	Young, single; young, married, no children; young, married with children; older, married with children; older, married, no children under 18; older, single; other
Income	Under $10,000; $10,000-$20,000; $20,000-$30,000; $30,000-$50,000; $50,000-$100,000; $100,000+
Occupation	Professional and technical; managers, officials, and proprietors; clerical, sales; craftspeople; foremen; operatives; farmers; retired; students; homemakers; unemployed
Education	Grade school or less; some high school; high school graduate; some college; college graduate
Religion	Catholic, Protestant, Jewish, Muslim, Hindu, other
Race	Asian, Hispanic, black, white
Nationality	North American, South American, British, French, German, Italian, Japanese
PSYCHOGRAPHIC	
Social class	Lower lowers, upper lowers, working class, middle class, upper middles, lower uppers, upper uppers
Lifestyle	Achievers, strivers, strugglers
Personality	Compulsive, gregarious, authoritarian, ambitious
BEHAVIORAL	
Occasions	Regular occasion, special occasion
Benefits	Quality, service, economy, convenience, speed
User status	Nonuser, ex-user, potential user, first-time user, regular user
Usage rate	Light user, medium user, heavy user
Loyalty status	None, medium, strong, absolute
Readiness stage	Unaware, aware, informed, interested, desirous, intending to buy
Attitude toward product	Enthusiastic, positive, indifferent, negative, hostile

The activity of listing the goods and services of entities on the Market-Product Grid is quite simple, but identifying and listing potential markets can be somewhat challenging without some point of reference. This point of reference can often be found by consulting a breakdown of segmentation variables, such as the one listed in Table 10-1.

This chart provides examples of specific segments that exist within each of the four major segmentation categories: geographic, demographic, psychographic, and behavioral. It, however, presents only a few of the almost endless market segments that marketers could potentially pursue. Such a chart serves as a useful starting point for identifying markets for placement on the Market-Product Grid.

In Practice

Figure 10-2 illustrates a Market-Product Grid developed for a dry cleaning establishment. Here, the company used the Grid to assess

---

FIGURE 10-2: A Dry Cleaner's Market-Product Grid

Products / Markets	Dry Cleaning Services
North	1
South	3
East	2
West	1
Central	3

(Markets are grouped under **Jackson County**)

3 = Large Market, 2 = Medium Market, 1 = Small Market, 0 = No Market

the market potential of different areas of Jackson County. The Grid indicates that the South and Central sections of Jackson County possess large markets, the East section possesses a medium market, and the North and West sections contain small markets. The Grid clearly identifies the most prominent markets (South and Central regions) for dry cleaning services within the county—information that can greatly assist the company in determining which markets it wishes to pursue.

Figure 10-3 presents a more complex Market-Product Grid developed for an athletic outfitter. Here, the sports shop sought to examine Washington County's market potential for various sporting goods products by type of sport. The Grid notably reveals a prominent market across all sports for footwear, followed closely by nutrition products and training offerings. It also reveals that, among sports types, the Tennis and Golf sports populations possess the largest markets for broad sporting goods products—details that shed significant light on segment opportunities.

FIGURE 10-3: An Athletic Outfitter's Market-Product Grid

Products / Markets	Sporting Goods Products					
	Apparel	Footwear	Equipment	Training	Nutrition	Gifts
Football Players	1	1	0	1	2	0
Basketball Players	1	2	0	1	1	0
Baseball Players	0	1	1	1	1	0
Soccer Players	1	2	0	1	2	1
Tennis Players	3	3	2	2	3	2
Golfers	2	3	2	3	1	2

(Left axis label: Washington County)

3 = Large Market, 2 = Medium Market, 1 = Small Market, 0 = No Market

It should be noted that although it may seem that the obvious choice would be to select the largest markets to pursue, such a decision is not always most appropriate. Organizations must, for example, factor in marketplace competitors, their dominance in certain segments, and their overall numbers. Certain segments, although large, may be saturated with competitors or dominated by market leaders. In such situations, smaller markets with fewer competitors may be more desirable segments to pursue.

Aside from competitive elements, business entities may select smaller markets based on the particular missions they embrace. Entities that cater to rural markets represent excellent examples of institutions engaging in this practice.

It should also be noted that Market-Product Grids are only as accurate as the information that is used to complete them. Although they remain useful even with informally collected data, the use of data derived from formal market research can greatly improve their accuracy.

In Summary

The Market-Product Grid provides a simple, yet highly useful, method for segmenting and targeting markets. By using this tool, marketers can more precisely identify and target appropriate customer groups. The Market-Product Grid also ensures that marketers consider multiple market opportunities.

REFERENCES:

Berkowitz, Eric N., Roger A. Kerin, Steven W. Hartley, and William Rudelius. *Marketing.* 6th ed. New York: McGraw-Hill, 2000.

Kotler, Philip, and Gary Armstrong. *Principles of Marketing.* 8th ed. Upper Saddle River, NJ: Prentice Hall, 1999.

PHILIP KOTLER'S
SEGMENT-BY-SEGMENT INVASION PLAN

11

When growth-minded business marketers engage in target marketing, they not only identify segments that they wish to immediately pursue, but they also identify segments that they might target in the future. In essence, they formulate plans that outline current and future market segment pursuits. This practice is beneficial due to the fact that all market segments, if successfully pursued, will eventually be exhausted of growth opportunities for given product offerings. By proactively identifying future market segments to pursue, marketers are better prepared to embark on a course of sustained growth.

The practice of identifying future segment pursuits is greatly facilitated by using Philip Kotler's Segment-by-Segment Invasion Plan which, as illustrated in Figure 11-1, consists of a vertical axis representing product varieties and a horizontal axis representing customer groups. Each of the resulting cells in the matrix identifies market segments that are available to pursue, with the actual number of cells being dependent, of course, on the number of product varieties and customer groups identified.

To create an Invasion Plan, marketers simply (1) construct a matrix of sufficient size, (2) list product varieties on the vertical axis, (3) list customer groups on the horizontal axis, (4) identify, using unique hatch patterns, the organizations (including their own) that are currently pursuing the segments formed in the matrix, and (5) identify, using arrows, the segments that they wish to pursue in the future. The resulting Segment-by-Segment Invasion Plan provides marketers with a concise self and competitive assessment of current market segment pursuits. It also illustrates the anticipated future market segment pursuits of the evaluating organization.

In Practice

Figure 11-2 illustrates a Segment-by-Segment Invasion Plan that was developed for Family Restaurants, a restaurant corporation. The diagram indicates that Family Restaurants is operating hamburger restaurants in the Southtown and Midtown markets, Quality Eateries is operating both fried chicken restaurants and pizza restaurants in the Northtown market, and Star Pizzerias is operating pizza restaurants in the Northtown, Midtown, and Southtown markets.

Seeking increased growth, Family Restaurants is planning to expand its geographic reach by opening a hamburger restaurant in the Northtown market. If successful, the restaurant corporation plans to diversify its product array by opening a fried chicken restaurant in the Northtown

---

FIGURE 11-1: Kotler's Segment-by-Segment Invasion Plan

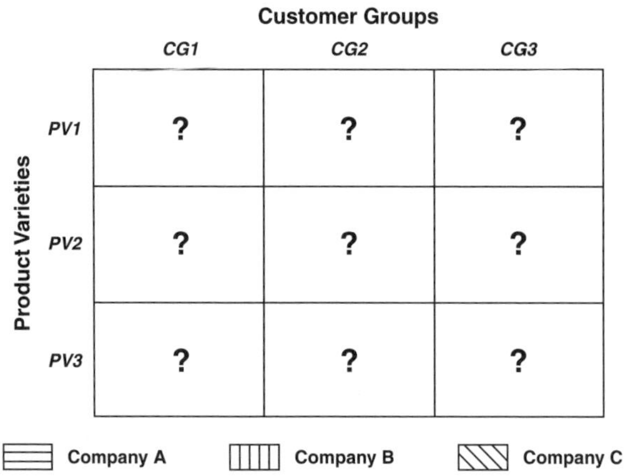

Adapted from MARKETING MANAGEMENT: THE MILLENNIUM EDITION 10/E by Kotler, Philip. © 2000. Reprinted by permission of Pearson Education, Inc., Upper Saddle River, NJ.

FIGURE 11-2: A Restaurant Corporation's Invasion Plan

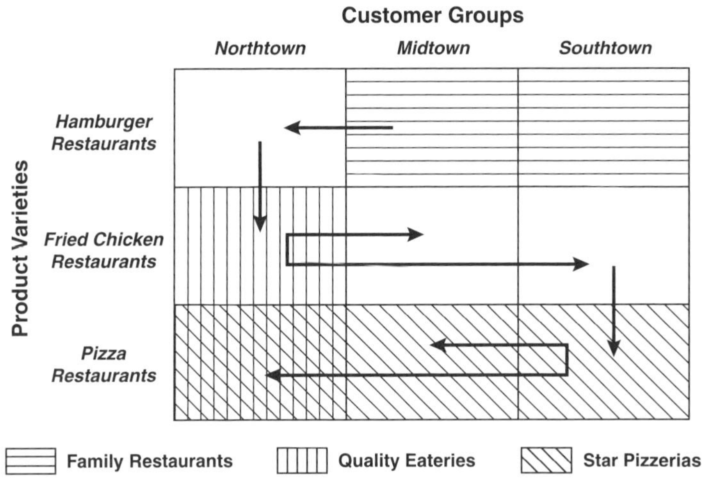

Adapted from MARKETING MANAGEMENT: THE MILLENNIUM EDITION 10/E by Kotler, Philip. © 2000. Reprinted by permission of Pearson Education, Inc., Upper Saddle River, NJ.

market which will be followed by simultaneous entries into the Midtown and Southtown markets. If the fried chicken restaurant ventures are successful, Family Restaurants plans to further diversify its product portfolio by opening a pizza restaurant in the Southtown market which will be followed by simultaneous entries into the Midtown and Northtown markets.

With this information, marketers at Family Restaurants have a concise portrayal of the current market segment pursuits of identified competitors. These marketers also possess a useful depiction of the market segments that Family Restaurants might pursue in the future.

Beyond the depiction of current and future segment pursuits, Kotler's Segment-by-Segment Invasion Plan affords marketers with the opportunity to formulate marketing strategies and tactics associated with their growth pursuits. Marketers can, for example, assess barriers to entry, evaluate competitors, predict competitive responses to invasions, and assess segment limitations. By proactively addressing the requirements of upcoming segment invasions, marketers increase the likelihood that their pursuits will be successful.

It should be noted that marketers must ensure that their Segment-by-Segment Invasion Plans are kept strictly confidential. The element of surprise is essential for any segment invasion. If competitors gain access to this information, the element of surprise is, of course, eliminated. This allows competitors the opportunity to take preemptive actions to defend themselves against anticipated segment invasions, making invasions much more difficult or even impossible.

In Summary

Despite success in particular market segments, marketers must understand that every segment possesses growth boundaries. Therefore, if marketers and their organizations desire sustained growth, they must identify and pursue new markets and market segments—a task facilitated by Kotler's Segment-by-Segment Invasion Plan. Usefully, this tool forces marketers to identify future segment pursuits that will yield sustained organizational performance.

REFERENCE:

Kotler, Philip. *Marketing Management: The Millennium Edition.* 10th ed. Upper Saddle River, NJ: Prentice Hall, 2000.

THE PERCEPTUAL MAP

12

Target marketing is an essential practice involving three interrelated activities: market segmentation, targeting, and product positioning. Market segmentation is the process of dividing a market into groups (segments) of individuals who share common characteristics. Once the market has been segmented, marketers engage in targeting where they select (target) attractive segments and focus their efforts on satisfying the wants and needs of these groups. After segmenting and targeting activities have been completed, marketers then position their products.

Product positioning involves the determination of an appropriate and effective "image" for products to convey to customers. An automobile manufacturer, for example, might wish to convey an image of top performance, while another might desire an image of safety and comfort. An aspirin manufacturer might wish to portray its product as an instant pain reliever, while another might emphasize the affordability of its product. A law firm might wish to emphasize its prestigious legal staff, while another might convey its convenient service. Once determined, marketers formulate methods to convey the desired product "imagery" to target markets through advertising, personal selling, sales promotion, and other means.

Once products have been positioned, marketers must monitor consumer perceptions related to the offerings to ensure that associated goods and services are perceived in the manner desired. A useful tool that provides

FIGURE 12-1: The Perceptual Map

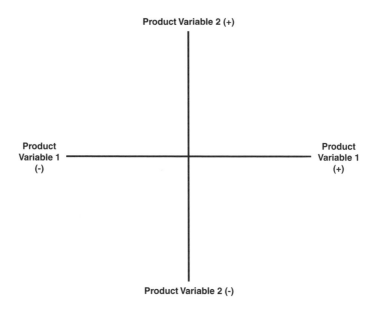

guidance to marketers in this endeavor is known as the Perceptual (or Positioning) Map which, as illustrated in Figure 12-1, consists of two intersected axes which represent different product-related attributes. When completed, a Perceptual Map demonstrates how consumers perceive products based on designated product attributes—information that is essential for the purposes of product positioning.

To assess products using the Perceptual Map, marketers (1) identify the offerings to be evaluated, (2) construct the Map diagram as illustrated in Figure 12-1, (3) determine the product-related attributes that will compose the Map's axes, labeling the diagram accordingly, (4) gather data pertaining to the consumer perceptions of products to be evaluated, and (5) plot the coordinates of each product on the Perceptual Map. This visual representation is then analyzed to determine if product offerings are perceived in the manner desired, allowing marketers to make adjustments as necessary to elicit desired perceptions. For increased insights into consumer perceptions, marketers can add competitive products to the Perceptual Map.

In Practice

Figure 12-2 illustrates a Perceptual Map that was completed by a bank. Here, the bank sought to evaluate consumer perceptions regarding its array of financial services in relation to competitive offerings on the basis of personal service (more or less) and convenience (more or less). The diagram indicates that one bank is perceived to offer more personal and more convenient service, three banks (including the evaluating bank) are perceived to offer more personal but less convenient service, four banks are perceived to offer less personal and less convenient service, and two banks are perceived to offer less personal but more convenient service. Of course, by examining each quadrant, more specific information can be obtained. The evaluating bank is, for example, viewed as the most personal of the three banks in the "more personal, less convenient" quadrant, but the least convenient of the three.

FIGURE 12-2: A Bank's Perceptual Map

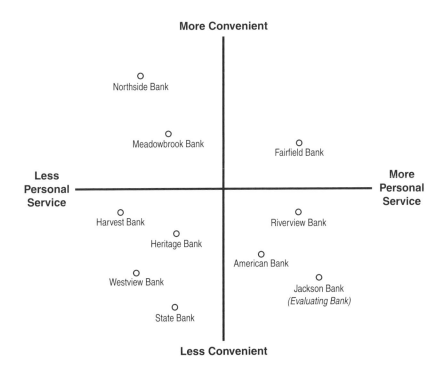

With the information provided by the Perceptual Map, the bank could take steps to improve the manner in which it is perceived. Since the facility was viewed negatively in the area of convenient service, the bank might consider introducing measures to increase convenience, such as better parking and extended hours. Of course, the bank could gain even greater insights into its operation by completing additional Perceptual Maps to view consumer perceptions regarding other product attributes.

Exploratory Perceptual Maps

Beyond assessing current products, Perceptual Maps are also useful for positioning new or anticipated product offerings. Figure 12-3 identifies an Exploratory Perceptual Map that was completed by a hotel properties management corporation seeking to assess expansion opportunities in a particular community. Here, the corporation assessed the community's existing hotel properties based on amenities (many or few) and price (high or low). The completed Exploratory Perceptual Map indicates that three hotels are perceived to offer many amenities at a high price, one hotel is perceived to offer few amenities at a low price, and one hotel is perceived to offer few amenities at a high price.

With this Map, the corporation has an enhanced perspective of the hotel properties market in the community which can guide it in determining how it might possibly enter the market. Notably, the diagram illustrates that a void exists in the market's "many amenities, low price" quadrant. This void may represent an opportunity for the hotel corporation to differentiate itself from existing competitors by establishing the community's only hotel that offers many amenities at a low price. The Exploratory Perceptual Map also allows the hotel corporation to assess various competitive approaches to hotel properties management.

Other Points

It is important to remember that Perceptual Maps are only as accurate as the information that is used to complete them. In constructing these

Maps, some marketers simply use their own judgement regarding consumer perceptions related to the product offerings under evaluation. Others assemble groups consisting of members of their product management teams to discuss likely consumer perceptions, developing Perceptual Maps accordingly. Still other marketers use formal market research to construct these Maps. Although Perceptual Maps remain useful even with informally collected data, the use of data derived from formal market research can greatly improve their accuracy.

It is also important to remember that Perceptual Maps do indeed deal with perceptions. Consumer perceptions, of course, change over time, a fact which necessitates that marketers routinely construct and analyze Perceptual Maps in an effort to stay abreast of the latest consumer perceptions regarding product offerings.

FIGURE 12-3: A Hotel's Exploratory Perceptual Map

In Summary

The Perceptual Map provides marketers with a helpful tool for under-standing consumer perceptions related to product offerings. Usefully, the Perceptual Map can be employed to assess consumer perceptions related to both current and anticipated product offerings. Such infor-mation greatly assists marketers in their ongoing product positioning responsibilities, making the Perceptual Map an indispensable market-ing tool.

THE RIES & TROUT PRODUCT LADDER

13

Given that marketers ultimately seek to effect exchanges with target markets, they must constantly focus on the manner in which consumers perceive their products in relation to competitive offerings. Ideally, marketers would like for their goods and services, rather than those of competitors, to be viewed most favorably by consumers. Achieving such prominent positions in the minds of consumers is indeed a difficult task, but if attained, yields significant benefits.

For insights into attaining such lofty positions in the minds of consumers, marketers frequently refer to the Product Ladder, a useful tool developed by Al Ries and Jack Trout. Illustrated in Figure 13-1, the Product Ladder consists of an outline of a human head, representing a consumer's mind, with a ladder situated inside, representing the consumer's rank order of brands within a particular product category.

Ries and Trout developed the Product Ladder to illustrate that, given the limitations of the human mind coupled with the proliferation of available goods and services, consumers are forced to rank products in their minds.

These rankings can be depicted as a series of ladders in the minds of consumers, with each ladder representing a different product category and each step representing a different product brand. Products situated on higher steps rank higher in the minds of consumers than products situated on lower steps.

Product Ladders may consist of as few as one step to many steps, although ladders with seven or more steps are considered to be quite lengthy. Product Ladders are also consumer-specific—they are based on the particular views of given individuals.

Some consumers may not be aware of brands within particular product categories and would, therefore, not possess associated Product Ladders. Consumers who, for example, have never had a need for a lawyer may not possess a Product Ladder for legal services. When consumers develop needs for unfamiliar goods and services, however, Product Ladders form rather quickly as consumers actively solicit information regarding given product offerings through both formal and informal channels.

In Practice

To assess products using the Product Ladder, marketers simply (1) identify the product category to be evaluated, (2) gather data pertain-

---

FIGURE 13-1: The Ries & Trout Product Ladder

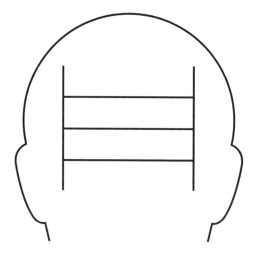

FIGURE 13-2: A Series of Completed Product Ladders

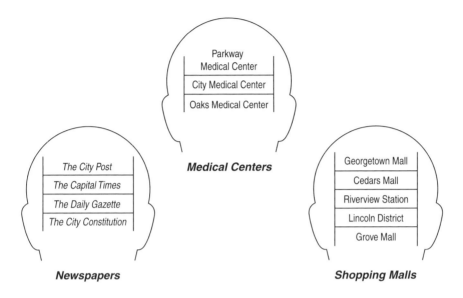

Adapted from *Positioning: The Battle for Your Mind*, 20th anniversary ed. by Al Ries and Jack Trout. Copyright © 2001, 1981 by The McGraw-Hill Companies, Inc. Published by McGraw-Hill. Reproduced with permission of The McGraw-Hill Companies.

ing to the consumer perceptions of product brands within the identified category, and (3) construct a Product Ladder that is representative of the findings. This visual representation is then analyzed to gain product insights.

Figure 13-2 presents a series of Product Ladders illustrating a particular consumer's perceptions regarding a variety of product offerings, namely newspapers, medical centers, and shopping malls. The products occupying the top rungs of these ladders represent those offerings that, in their respective product categories, the consumer views as most favorable. Products at lower levels, however, are not as highly regarded by the consumer.

Of course, these particular Product Ladders represent the perceptions of only one individual whose views may or may not coincide with prevailing perceptions in the market. Marketers seeking more extensive and, thus, useful perspectives of consumer perceptions would need to acquire representative samples of product rankings for given product categories from targeted consumers. The data could then be aggregated and used to construct "market representative" Product Ladders that marketers could, in turn, use to determine strategic and tactical priorities.

Moving Up the Product Ladder

Marketers whose products occupy lower-level positions face an extremely difficult challenge as they pursue the top steps of Product Ladders. Although the outright dislodging of top-rung brands is usually impossible, marketers can make inroads toward these positions by relating their products to market leading offerings.

A newly established department store, for example, might feature in its advertisements its enhanced array of products in relation to the market's leading retailer. A pharmaceutical manufacturer might tout in its advertisements that its pain reliever works faster than the leading product. Sales representatives for a computer manufacturer might tout their product line's enhanced performance, increased upgradeability, better warranty, and more comprehensive customer support policy relative to the market leader's offerings. By relating lower-rung products to market leading offerings, marketers exploit consumer familiarity to leverage their own product positions.

New Products & the Product Ladder

It should be mentioned that when marketers introduce *new-to-the-world products*, those products that define entirely new product categories never before offered to the public, consumers must formulate new Product Ladders in their minds. Marketers can assist consumers in the construction of these new ladders by relating totally new product offerings to existing products. Ries and Trout note that this approach was used with the introduction of the automobile which was initially referred to as a "horseless" carriage, allowing consumers a familiar point of reference to understand and evaluate the new-to-the-world product offering. Once again, marketers exploit familiarity to gain a foothold in the minds of consumers.

In Summary

The Ries and Trout Product Ladder provides marketers with a useful tool for understanding the manner in which consumers perceive products in relation to competitive offerings. Notably, this tool directs attention to the fact that consumers rank products in their minds, with higher rankings indicating more favorable product offerings. The useful insights generated by the Product Ladder provide great assistance to marketers in their endeavors to achieve prominent positions for their product offerings in the minds of consumers.

REFERENCE:

Ries, Al, and Jack Trout. *Positioning: The Battle for Your Mind.* 20th anniversary ed. New York: McGraw-Hill, 2001.

PART THREE

CONSUMER BEHAVIOR
&
PRODUCT PROMOTIONS TOOLS

ABRAHAM MASLOW'S
HIERARCHY OF NEEDS

14

Motivations to purchase and consume products are as complex and varied as the number of available goods and services in the marketplace. These motivations are fueled by an equally complex and varied array of human wants and needs which marketers seek to address through the development and distribution of goods and services.

Different issues, circumstances, and events spark different motivations which require different interventions (i.e., goods and services). Given this, it is essential for marketers to possess a thorough understanding of human motivation.

One leading theory of human motivation was developed by Abraham Maslow who theorized that all human needs can be grouped into one of five hierarchical categories (physiological, safety, social, esteem, and self-actualization) and that needs at one level will not motivate a person until needs at the preceding level have been satisfied. In other words, physiological needs must be satisfied before safety needs will become motivators, safety needs must be satisfied before social needs will become motivators, social needs must be satisfied before esteem needs will become motivators, and so on.

Illustrated in Figure 14-1, Maslow's Hierarchy of Needs is depicted as a pyramid consisting of five hierarchical levels representing different categories of human needs. These categories, accompanied by various industry examples, are identified as follows:

Physiological Needs

Physiological needs represent basic human needs that are required for survival including air, food, water, and health. Although industrialized societies have made significant progress in reducing the incidence of thirst and starvation, many products address physiological needs in manners beyond simple survival.

Fast food restaurants with menus that offer, say, healthy foods are excellent examples of companies seeking to address the physiological needs of consumers. Nourishing food products on grocery store shelves (e.g., low fat, reduced sodium, preservative-free, and related items) address physiological needs as well. The same would be true of bottled water companies offering purified water to customers.

Other products that address physiological needs include tap water filtration systems, home air purifiers, and, significantly, the gamut of healthcare goods and services, ranging from physical examinations provided by physicians to pharmaceutical products manufactured by various drug companies. All of these offerings target the physiological needs of consumers.

Safety Needs

Safety needs represent human needs for security and protection. Health and life insurance products are excellent examples of items that address the safety and security needs of individuals. The same would be true of burglar alarms and related security systems that electronically protect homes and their occupants. Storm shelters, smoke detectors, deadbolts and padlocks, and automobile airbags could be viewed in an equivalent light. These products offer individuals the peace of mind of knowing that they are protected.

Social Needs

Social needs involve human needs for love, friendship, affiliation, and acceptance by others. Products that address the social needs of individuals are quite varied and include such items as greeting cards and stationery to correspond with loved ones, cellular and landline telephones and associated services to communicate with friends, and memberships in various civic, professional, and fraternal organizations. All of these products facilitate social interaction.

Esteem Needs

Esteem needs represent human needs for pride, prestige, attention, and recognition from others. Luxury automobiles are excellent examples of products that address esteem needs. The same would be true of elaborate homes, expensive jewelry, yacht club memberships, and exclusive vacation getaways. These products represent only a few of the many goods and services that individuals with the requisite funds purchase,

---

FIGURE 14-1: Maslow's Hierarchy of Needs

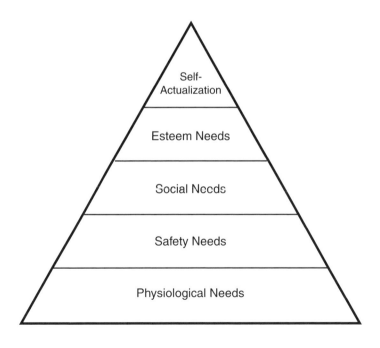

From *The Maslow Business Reader* by Abraham H. Maslow, edited by Deborah C. Stephens. Copyright © 2000 by Ann R. Kaplan. Reprinted by permission of John Wiley & Sons, Inc.

often as a means of increasing their self-confidence, pride in themselves, and appeal to others.

Self-Actualization Needs

Self-actualization needs represent human needs for personal growth and fulfillment and the marketplace offers rich opportunities for individuals to satisfy these desires. Donations of time (through volunteerism) and money (through financial contributions) to educational institutions, community groups, and charitable organizations are examples of marketplace opportunities that allow individuals to fulfill self-actualization needs. When individuals reach this level, they are operating at their pinnacle.

In Practice

Maslow's Hierarchy of Needs is perhaps most useful to marketers as a tool for conceptualizing the underlying wants and needs (collectively termed "needs" by Maslow) that drive consumption of goods and services. By possessing a better understanding of the wants and needs satisfied by particular products, the underlying associated motivations, and the hierarchical order of the corresponding needs categories, marketers are better prepared to formulate promotional campaigns and engage in ongoing product management responsibilities.

Although Maslow theorized that higher level needs will not motivate individuals until lower level needs have been satisfied, he acknowledged that variations are possible and do occur. One could easily envision a situation where a person might decide to purchase an expensive piece of jewelry (an esteem need) instead of an adequate life insurance policy (a safety need). This example illustrates that, among individuals, priorities often differ and may lead to unique pursuits.

In Summary

Maslow's Hierarchy of Needs serves as a simple, yet highly effective, tool for understanding human motivation. This tool is particularly useful in today's marketplace where motivations to consume the seemingly endless array of goods and services are driven by an equally intensive array of wants and needs.

Quite obviously, marketers can greatly improve marketing results if they understand how their product offerings "fit" into the overall scheme of human motivation. By understanding human motivation, marketers can better devise promotional campaigns that emphasize the attributes of associated product offerings in the context of the wants and needs that motivate purchase and consumption, thus increasing the likelihood of marketing success.

REFERENCE:

Maslow, Abraham H. *The Maslow Business Reader*, edited by Deborah C. Stephens. New York: Wiley, 2000.

15

EVERETT ROGERS' DIFFUSION OF INNOVATIONS MODEL

Product innovations, new goods and services that significantly enhance or improve one or more aspects of life, are usually not adopted by all members of a targeted market simultaneously. Instead, acceptance of these new products occurs gradually over time, a process referred to as *diffusion*. Emergent situations aside, consumers vary in their willingness to adopt new products. Some are quick to embrace new offerings, while others are less inclined to do so. Those who eagerly accept new products possess characteristics that are different from those who delay adoption. To understand the unique characteristics of adopters and their levels of innovativeness, marketers frequently turn to Everett Rogers' Diffusion of Innovations Model.

Illustrated in Figure 15-1, Rogers' Diffusion of Innovations Model is depicted as a bell-shaped curve that represents the adoption of an innovation over time. The model categorizes individuals as innovators, early adopters, early majority, late majority, or laggards based on when they adopt an innovation. These adopter categories are described as follows:

Innovators

Described as "venturesome," innovators represent the first 2.5 percent of adopters. These individuals are comfortable with risk and uncertainty and are also typically wealthy—a prerequisite given that they must have the ability to absorb losses in the event that innovations fail to meet expectations. Although they are rarely community opinion leaders, innovators are instrumental in the diffusion process because of their willingness to quickly adopt new goods and services. Their initial usage experiences indirectly promote innovations to other consumers in the market, building product awareness and ultimately hastening the diffusion process.

Early Adopters

Early adopters are characterized by "respect" and make up the next 13.5 percent of adopters. They are community opinion leaders who command the respect of their peers—peers who look to these early adopters for advice on whether they, too, should adopt innovations. Early adopters serve as information disseminators in that, upon adoption of product offerings, they are quick to convey their experiences to others. Given these characteristics, it is quite obvious that early adopters play an essential role in the diffusion process.

Early Majority

Members of the early majority are described as "deliberate" and represent the next 34 percent of adopters. These individuals are rarely

---

FIGURE 15-1: Rogers' Diffusion of Innovations Model

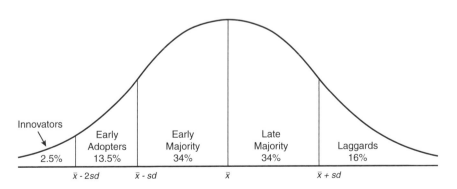

opinion leaders, but do actively interact with their peers. They tend to deliberate for some time before they adopt new products. Early majority members do not want to be the first or the last to adopt innovations.

Late Majority

Members of the late majority are described as "skeptical" and make up the next 34 percent of adopters. These cautious individuals are skeptical of new ideas and often only adopt innovations under peer pressure. Their reluctance to adopt innovations is related to their relatively scarce resources—a factor which necessitates that late majority members delay adoption until new product uncertainties are removed.

Laggards

Laggards are described as "traditional" and represent the last 16 percent of adopters. These individuals are suspicious of new products and are highly resistant to change of any kind. They are almost never opinion leaders and have very limited marketplace interactions. Like members of the late majority, laggards possess few resources—a factor that reduces their willingness to adopt innovations until new product uncertainties are eliminated.

In Practice

Research suggests that differences between earlier and later adopters are quite pronounced, as illustrated in Table 15-1. By targeting earlier adopters, those who more quickly adopt innovations, significant new product publicity can be generated through their extensive informal networks. This increased (and free) publicity, of course, acts to hasten the innovation diffusion process, making earlier adopters very desirable targets for cost-conscious marketers seeking to maximize their promotions resources.

Of course, there are situations in the marketplace where instant innovation adoption would be expected. Many innovations are consumed not out of desire, but out of need which tends to hasten the diffusion process. Individuals suffering from debilitating illnesses, for example, would likely immediately adopt a pharmaceutical innovation that offered hope for recovery. Likewise, individuals left stranded by an inoperable automobile would hardly discourage the receipt of innovative repair services.

Innovation adoption can also be hastened by governmental regulations that encourage or mandate the adoption of new technologies for the benefit of society (e.g., energy-efficient air conditioning systems, biodegradable paper products, automobiles with features that enhance safety). Clearly, such circumstances and events act as innovation adoption catalysts.

TABLE 15-1: Differences Between Earlier & Later Adopters

- Earlier adopters have more years of formal education than later adopters.

- Earlier adopters have higher social status than later adopters.

- Earlier adopters have a greater degree of upward social mobility than later adopters.

- Earlier adopters have greater intelligence than later adopters.

- Earlier adopters have a more favorable attitude toward change than later adopters.

- Earlier adopters are better able to cope with uncertainty and risk than later adopters.

- Earlier adopters have a more favorable attitude toward science than later adopters.

- Earlier adopters are more highly interconnected through interpersonal networks in their social system than later adopters.

- Earlier adopters are more cosmopolite than later adopters.

- Earlier adopters have greater exposure to mass media communications channels than later adopters.

- Earlier adopters seek information about innovations more actively than later adopters.

- Earlier adopters have a higher degree of opinion leadership than later adopters.

Derived from information in *Diffusion of Innovations*, 4th ed. by Everett M. Rogers. New York: The Free Press, 1995: 268-274.

In Summary

The innovation-rich business marketplace necessitates that marketers possess a thorough understanding of the innovation diffusion process. Rogers' Diffusion of Innovations Model yields significant insights into the unique characteristics of adopters and their levels of innovativeness. This tool allows marketers to better understand their customers and more effectively design promotional campaigns that expedite the innovation diffusion process.

REFERENCE:

Rogers, Everett M. *Diffusion of Innovations.* 4th ed. New York: The Free Press, 1995.

The DAGMAR Marketing Communications Spectrum

16

Society has become reliant on the seemingly endless array of innovations that routinely enter the marketplace. Such innovations have not only become commonplace, but they also have become expected and even demanded by the public. The extensive range of innovative goods and services is simply overwhelming, with new innovations constantly entering the marketplace.

It might seem as though commercial success would be guaranteed simply by developing and providing new and improved goods and services. However, an equally important prerequisite for commercial success involves the successful communication of new offerings to potential customers. If customers are not aware of new and improved products, one could hardly expect the offerings to achieve commercial success.

New and improved goods and services can and do fail, often as a result of failed communications efforts. Clearly, marketers must endeavor to use good communicative techniques in their attempts to build consumer awareness of their product offerings.

The Mechanics of Communication

The awareness building process is a process of communication, an aspect of product management that falls under the promotions component of the marketing mix. Successes in promotion are the direct result of successes in communication. As illustrated in Figure

FIGURE 16-1: The Communications Process

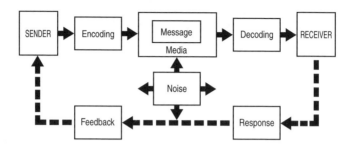

From MARKETING MANAGEMENT: THE MILLENNIUM EDITION 10/E by Kotler, Philip. © 2000. Reprinted by permission of Pearson Education, Inc., Upper Saddle River, NJ.

16-1, the communications process involves two parties: a sender and a receiver. The sender's objective is to deliver his or her intended message to the receiver. To do this, the sender encodes the message which is sent via selected media—the communications channel or channels through which the message is delivered—to the receiver. The receiver then decodes the message and, if inclined to do so, encodes a response which is returned to the sender as feedback. Feedback from the receiver may take many forms including requests for additional information, acceptances or rejections of sales proposals, and purchases of goods and services.

Throughout the communications process, message distortion and/or elimination may occur due to negative environmental influences collectively referred to as noise (e.g., competitive messages, physical distractions). Although the communications process seems quite simple, in reality it is among the most complex of processes and must be mastered for marketing success. Clearly, the ability of marketers to successfully communicate with current and potential customers greatly improves the marketplace experiences of associated product offerings.

The DAGMAR Marketing Communications Spectrum

When consumers adopt new products, the act of adoption is rarely a singular event. Singularity of the process would not be expected, of course, because consumers must minimally gain familiarity with new product offerings, determining, among other things, the potential benefits that might be offered by the associated goods and services. Instead, adoption consists of a series of progressive steps leading up to the purchase and consumption of new products.

To understand the adoption process, marketers frequently turn to the DAGMAR Marketing Communications Spectrum. (DAGMAR is an acronym for *Defining Advertising Goals for Measured Advertising Results*, the title of the book that presents the Spectrum.) Illustrated in Figure 16-2, the DAGMAR Marketing Communications Spectrum divides the adoption process into five sequential levels or stages, namely unawareness, awareness, comprehension, conviction, and action.

Each of these stages is influenced by marketing forces and countervailing forces, which are depicted by arrows in the diagram. The stages of the DAGMAR Marketing Communications Spectrum are explained as follows:

FIGURE 16-2: The DAGMAR Spectrum

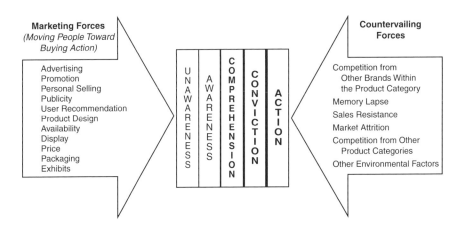

From *DAGMAR: Defining Advertising Goals for Measured Advertising Results*, 2d ed. by Solomon Dutka. (1st ed. by Russell Colley). Copyright © 1995 by NTC Publishing Group. Published by NTC Business Books. Reproduced with permission of The McGraw-Hill Companies.

Stage I: Unawareness

During the unawareness stage, consumers are oblivious to the existence of new goods and services. Any promotional messages that have been disseminated have not successfully reached consumers.

Stage II: Awareness

Consumers first become aware of the existence of new products during the awareness stage. Here, they also gain a general understanding of the potential benefits associated with new offerings. At this point, consumers possess a base level of knowledge regarding new products but little more. They cannot recall, for example, the entities that produce and provide the offerings, associated locations of availability, and so on.

Stage III: Comprehension

During the comprehension stage, consumers gain a detailed understanding of new products. Consumers are able to recall, for example, the entities that produce and provide the offerings, associated features and benefits, locations of availability, packaging, brand names, and logos.

Stage IV: Conviction

During the conviction stage, consumers develop strong beliefs regarding the virtues of new products. Here, preferences for new offerings are formulated. Consumers have filtered through the information gained from prior stages of the Spectrum and have become reasonably confident that the associated products will meet or exceed their expectations.

Stage V: Action

The DAGMAR Marketing Communications Spectrum concludes with the action stage where consumers decide to adopt (purchase and consume) new product offerings.

FIGURE 16-3: The Promotions Mix

Encouraging Action

Beyond identification of the stages of adoption, the DAGMAR Marketing Communications Spectrum illustrates the influences that marketing forces and countervailing forces have on consumers throughout the adoption process. Marketing forces (e.g., product design, pricing, advertising, personal selling, publicity) seek to move consumers toward action, while countervailing forces (e.g., competition, memory lapse, sales resistance, market attrition) seek to drive consumers away from action. Marketers must strive to develop promotional campaigns that will effectively neutralize countervailing forces and move consumers toward action in as expeditious a fashion as possible.

The exact composition of any promotional campaign is, of course, dependent on the specific nature of the products being marketed. In their quest to entice target markets to purchase and consume products, marketers normally promote goods and services using a variety of methods.

The array of methods used by marketers to communicate product information to customers is referred to as the promotions, or communications, mix which is identified in Figure 16-3 and defined in Table 16-1. Advertising tends to be used universally by all types of business entities (e.g., banking institutions, computer manufacturers, department stores, restaurants). However, other forms of promotion tend to be used more heavily in certain industries (e.g., personal selling in the automobile, office equipment, pharmaceutical, and health insurance industries). Each promotional method possesses strengths and weaknesses and must be studied carefully to ensure a goodness of fit with the given products to be marketed.

Once promotional methods have been selected, marketers must make additional decisions, many of which are specific to particular promotions vehicles. Advertising, for example, involves a variety of unique points of consideration which Philip Kotler termed the Five Ms of Advertising (see Figure 16-4). Regardless of the communicative tools

---

TABLE 16-1: Promotions Mix Definitions & Examples

ADVERTISING	A promotional method involving the paid use of mass media to deliver messages.
	Examples include newspaper ads, magazine ads, television ads, radio ads, and billboards.
PERSONAL SELLING	A promotional method involving the use of a sales force to convey messages.
	For example, sales representatives.
SALES PROMOTION	A promotional method involving the use of incentives to stimulate consumer interest.
	Examples include discount coupons, free gifts, samples, and contests.
PUBLIC RELATIONS	A promotional method involving the use of publicity and other unpaid forms of promotion to deliver messages.
	Examples include press releases, open houses, facility tours, and educational seminars.
DIRECT MARKETING	A promotional method involving the delivery of messages directly to consumers.
	Examples include direct-mail marketing, telemarketing, and catalog marketing.

FIGURE 16-4: Kotler's Five Ms of Advertising

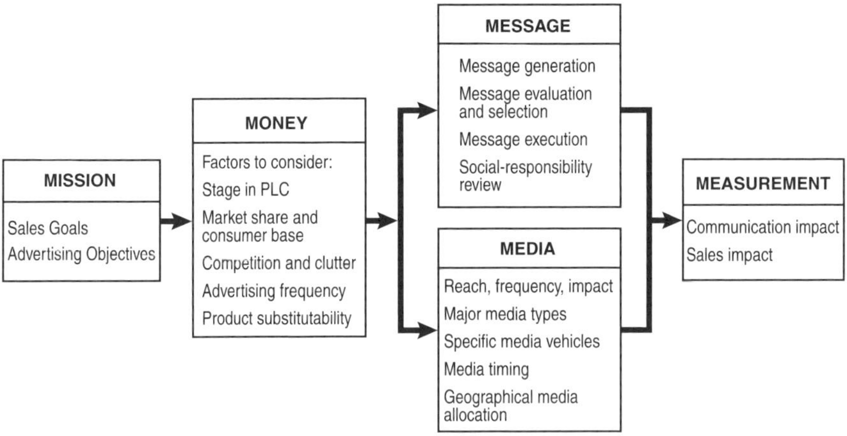

From MARKETING MANAGEMENT: THE MILLENNIUM EDITION 10/E by Kotler, Philip. © 2000. Reprinted by permission of Pearson Education, Inc., Upper Saddle River, NJ.

utilized, the goal of any promotions campaign is to move consumers through the successive stages of the DAGMAR Marketing Communications Spectrum as swiftly as possible.

Continued Product Use

It should be noted that although the DAGMAR Marketing Communications Spectrum concludes with product adoption, marketers must not neglect customers after the adoption decision. Continued use of product offerings by customers is as important as the initial adoption of the associated goods and services. Marketers must, therefore, strive to ensure that post-adoption attention is not neglected.

A hotel, for example, that provides poor service to a guest will likely lose the future business of this individual along with any personal referrals that would potentially be forwarded. An automobile dealer that neglects the wants and needs of a new vehicle owner will almost certainly lose the trust and the future business of this individual and possibly that of his or her network of friends, courtesy of negative word-of-mouth communications. Clearly, post-adoption support is imperative for enduring marketing success.

In Summary

The DAGMAR Marketing Communications Spectrum clearly illustrates the successive steps that consumers pass through toward the purchase and consumption of new goods and services, giving attention to the influences forwarded by marketing forces and countervailing forces. Among other things, the Spectrum serves as a useful reminder of the necessity to effectively communicate with target markets. Such effective communication acts to neutralize countervailing forces and move consumers toward action. The more expeditiously consumers move through the stages of the DAGMAR Marketing Communications Spectrum, the quicker the occurrence of exchange and resulting marketing success.

REFERENCES:

Dutka, Solomon. *DAGMAR: Defining Advertising Goals for Measured Advertising Results.* 2d ed. (1st ed. by Russell Colley). Lincolnwood, IL: NTC Business Books, 1995.

Kotler, Philip. *Marketing Management: The Millennium Edition.* 10th ed. Upper Saddle River, NJ: Prentice Hall, 2000.

THE RAPHEL & RAPHEL
LOYALTY LADDER

17

Business entities are ultimately dependent on customers and their continued patronage for survival, growth, and prosperity. Given this, marketers must focus significant attention on addressing the wants and needs of target markets through the provision of superior product solutions. When marketers select target markets, they must diligently pursue these groups in an effort to gain their patronage. Beyond individual transactions, however, marketers ideally seek to establish long-term relationships with their targeted audiences.

If marketers can gain a loyal following of customers, long-term success becomes a distinct possibility. Hence, marketers must possess a thorough understanding of loyalty and the methods for its attainment. To gain insight into the loyalty building process, marketers frequently refer to the Raphel and Raphel Loyalty Ladder.

Illustrated in Figure 17-1, the Raphel and Raphel Loyalty Ladder is depicted as a series of five steps (prospects, shoppers, customers, clients, and advocates) representing progressive levels of customer loyalty. The steps of the Loyalty Ladder are explained as follows:

Prospects

Individuals who might potentially have wants and needs for the goods and services of particular entities are considered prospects. At this step, individuals may or may not be aware of given entities and products. Regardless of this, however, purchase activity has not occurred.

A banking institution providing financial services to a community is immersed within an environment of prospects. The same could be said of a local restaurant that recently opened for business in the community or an automobile dealership which just received new models. Each of these entities must entice prospects to visit their establishments for current and future needs. To do this, marketers must convey the attributes of their various product offerings to consumers through the use of marketing communications (e.g., advertising, sales promotion, public relations).

Shoppers

Individuals who advance beyond the prospect stage and inquire about the goods and services offered by entities are considered shoppers. Shoppers have learned of organizations and associated product offerings and are debating extending their patronage.

People shop for both goods and services, albeit in different ways. The tangible nature of goods allows consumers to see and touch these offerings. Individuals can test drive new automobiles, taste test the latest soft drinks, and sample new soaps and detergents.

The intangible nature of services requires a slightly different shopping approach. Since these offerings cannot be seen or touched, individuals are more reliant on sales personnel and their descriptions of service delivery. Individuals might visit a new bank to learn of its various service offerings, visit a law office to discuss forthcoming legal matters, or attend an information seminar to learn about the home improvement services offered by a builder. If shoppers believe that the products under consideration will meet or exceed their expectations, they will advance to the next rung of the Loyalty Ladder—they become customers.

Customers

When individuals purchase and consume the goods and services offered by organizations, they become customers. Perhaps an individual test drives a new automobile and decides to purchase the vehicle.

With this person's purchase, the automobile dealer has gained a new customer. If the person has the automobile financed by the new bank in town, the bank, too, has gained a new customer. If these entities successfully meet and exceed the customer's expectations, the individual may become a repeat customer and graduate to the next rung of the Loyalty Ladder—the client.

Clients

Clients are those individuals who *regularly* purchase goods and services from given organizations. An individual who routinely has his or her clothing professionally cleaned by a particular dry cleaning establishment would be considered a client. The same would be said

---

FIGURE 17-1: The Raphel & Raphel Loyalty Ladder

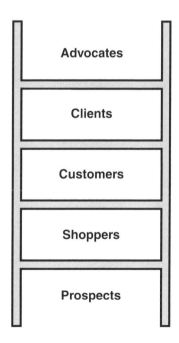

Adapted from *Up the Loyalty Ladder: Turning Sometime Customers into Full-Time Advocates of Your Business* by Murray Raphel and Neil Raphel. Copyright © 1995 by Neil Raphel and Murray Raphel. Published by HarperBusiness. Reprinted by permission of Murray Raphel.

of an individual who visits a particular grocery store weekly for his or her groceries or selects the same air carrier for any event requiring air transportation.

Importantly, business entities must not take the patronage of clients for granted. Organizations must ensure that they continue to offer the same high quality and service that originally converted customers into clients. Clients are extremely valuable to the entities they frequent. They become even more valuable if they can be converted into advocates.

Advocates

Advocates are individuals who have been so impressed with given establishments and associated product offerings that they openly encourage others to extend their patronage as well. If a client of a brokerage house, for example, openly communicates the virtues of the given establishment to co-workers, family members, and friends, the client becomes an advocate of the firm.

Advocates stand at the top of the Loyalty Ladder. They are the most valuable patrons of establishments for an obvious reason: Through their testimonies to others, advocates generate new patrons for entities.

In Practice

According to Raphel and Raphel, individuals are *always prospects, frequently shoppers, often customers, sometimes clients, and rarely advocates.* This statement succinctly illustrates that the more beneficial patrons, those occupying the top steps of the Loyalty Ladder, are not as common as their less valuable counterparts.

Fortunately, marketers can take steps to advance their customer base to higher levels of the Loyalty Ladder. This progression can be achieved by (1) producing and providing goods and services that meet and exceed the expectations of patrons and (2) embracing a customer service orientation that is championed by all employees.

Typical examples of activities that are likely to convert prospect
ultimately into advocates include operating clean and well-organized
facilities, providing the latest product innovations, and ensuring that
employees are helpful and courteous.

By engaging in these activities, business establishments are communicating to visitors that they are committed to excellence. Entities that
invest in institutional excellence will undoubtedly be rewarded by the
resulting loyalty of valuable patrons occupying the upper levels of the
Loyalty Ladder.

In Summary

The Raphel and Raphel Loyalty Ladder provides marketers with a useful
method for visualizing the progressive levels of customer loyalty. This
tool serves as a reminder of the need for business entities to produce
and provide top-quality goods and services, along with ever-increasing
levels of customer service, in an effort to boost individuals to progres-
sively higher and more prosperous rungs of the Loyalty Ladder.

REFERENCE:

Raphel, Murray, and Neil Raphel. *Up the Loyalty Ladder: Turning Sometime Customers into
Full-Time Advocates of Your Business.* New York: HarperBusiness, 1995.

The Osgood, Suci, & Tannenbaum Semantic Differential

Despite the multitude of activities that marketers perform, they are ultimately charged with satisfying the wants and needs of their target markets through the provision of effective product solutions. Given this, marketers must thoroughly understand customers and their perceptions regarding product offerings.

A useful tool for assessing customer perceptions related to product offerings is known as the Semantic Differential, an objective method for measurement developed by Charles Osgood, George Suci, and Percy Tannenbaum. The Semantic Differential is a broad-based measurement tool that can be implemented in a wide variety of fashions, depending on the associated research problems at hand. The broad-based nature of the Semantic Differential gives the tool enormous flexibility, but requires that it be adapted to given situations.

The Semantic Differential is best explained by viewing an example, such as the one identified in Figure 18-1 which seeks customer perceptions regarding a discount store. As depicted in Figure 18-1, the Semantic Differential is essentially a survey that presents a series of descriptive scales pertaining to perceptions associated with a particular good or service. The survey is distributed to customers or other applicable parties who are asked to judge the particular product based on the associated scales. Completed surveys are then averaged to reveal a single line, such as the one illustrated in Figure 18-2, which depicts the product perspectives of those who completed the survey.

The results of the discount store's survey, as depicted in Figure 18-2, clearly illustrate that the establishment is viewed very positively by its customer base in all areas except in regard to parking and hours of operation. With this information, the discount store can work to improve its performance in these areas. Parking might be improved by leasing adjacent property and constructing a new parking area. Hours of operation might be extended to better serve patrons of the discount store.

FIGURE 18-1: A Retailer's Semantic Differential Survey

What do you think?   **City Discount Store**

For each of the following scales, place an "X" in the blank that best reflects your views regarding the given attribute. When completed, please place the survey in one of our survey collection boxes.

Convenient location ___:___:___:___:___:___	Inconvenient location
Convenient parking ___:___:___:___:___:___	Inconvenient parking
Convenient hours ___:___:___:___:___:___	Inconvenient hours
Wide product selection ___:___:___:___:___:___	Narrow product selection
Low prices ___:___:___:___:___:___	High prices
Easy returns ___:___:___:___:___:___	Difficult returns
Clean facilities ___:___:___:___:___:___	Dirty facilities
Friendly employees ___:___:___:___:___:___	Unfriendly employees
Excellent customer service ___:___:___:___:___:___	Poor customer service

Thank you for your participation!

In Practice

Clearly, the Semantic Differential offers marketers a convenient method for assessing customer perceptions related to given product offerings. As illustrated in the previous example, this tool requires that marketers simply (1) formulate a series of scales related to a given offering, (2) prepare a survey depicting these scales, (3) distribute the survey to customers, and (4) average and illustrate survey results. The results

---

FIGURE 18-2: A Retailer's Semantic Differential Survey Results

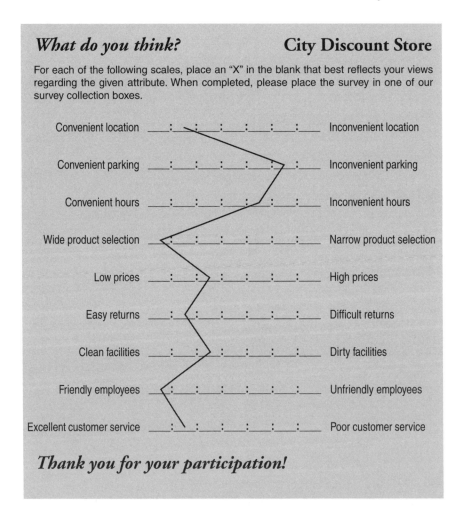

What do you think?   **City Discount Store**

For each of the following scales, place an "X" in the blank that best reflects your views regarding the given attribute. When completed, please place the survey in one of our survey collection boxes.

Convenient location	Inconvenient location
Convenient parking	Inconvenient parking
Convenient hours	Inconvenient hours
Wide product selection	Narrow product selection
Low prices	High prices
Easy returns	Difficult returns
Clean facilities	Dirty facilities
Friendly employees	Unfriendly employees
Excellent customer service	Poor customer service

Thank you for your participation!

of the Semantic Differential survey are then analyzed to determine the strengths and weaknesses associated with the product under evaluation.

In addition to its use as an assessment tool for the products held by entities, the Semantic Differential can also provide valuable insights into competitive offerings. Gaining this knowledge simply requires that marketers circulate an expanded survey that includes a section for respondents to complete concerning competitive products. If used in this fashion, the results can be respectively averaged and displayed on a single diagram, such as the one illustrated in Figure 18-3 which was developed to assess competing airlines in a market.

The results clearly indicate that Central Airlines, the evaluating entity, is perceived by survey respondents to be superior to Global Airlines in

FIGURE 18-3: Survey Results for Competing Airlines

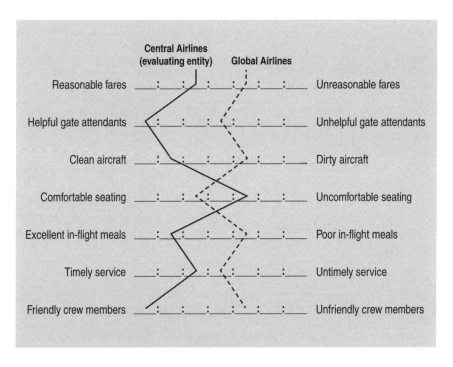

all areas with the exception of the passenger seating category, where it is viewed to offer less passenger comfort. With this information, Central Airlines can concentrate on addressing the passenger seating issue while maintaining the overwhelmingly positive attributes noted by respondents.

It should be noted that the Semantic Differential can also be used to monitor institutional progress. This is accomplished by circulating identical Semantic Differential surveys over time and comparing the results. By using the Semantic Differential in this manner, marketers gain even greater insights into their operations.

In Summary

The Semantic Differential provides marketers with a highly flexible tool for understanding how customers perceive product offerings. With this information, marketers can take steps to build upon product strengths and reduce or eliminate associated weaknesses. By gaining a better understanding of consumer perceptions regarding products, marketers are better equipped to offer goods and services that satisfy the wants and needs of target markets.

REFERENCE:

Osgood, Charles E., George J. Suci, and Percy H. Tannenbaum. *The Measurement of Meaning*. Urbana, IL: University of Illinois Press, 1957.

PART FOUR

ENVIRONMENTAL ANALYSIS
&
COMPETITIVE ASSESSMENT TOOLS

The PEST Analysis

Business entities exist in a much larger, macro-environment teeming with opportunities and threats capable of bolstering or destroying institutional progress. Although these environmental forces are beyond the control of those responsible for managing establishments, it is essential for marketers to actively monitor and evaluate these elements in an effort to capitalize on opportunities and avoid or eliminate threats.

A useful tool for performing this evaluative task is known as the PEST Analysis. This analysis, illustrated in Figure 19-1, involves the assessment of a series of macro-environmental variables (political, economic, social, and technological) that can potentially influence organizations. Political, economic, social, and technological forces are defined as follows:

Political Forces

Political forces involve all aspects associated with the legal and political framework of the environment. Quite obviously, political forces flow from those possessing such power, namely public officials (e.g., governors, legislators, judges) and the vast administrative bureaucracies charged with implementing and overseeing their initiatives (e.g., the Federal Deposit Insurance Corporation, the Food and Drug Administration, the Transportation Security Administration).

Political forces impact all industries, although many are industry-specific, with some industries receiving greater political scrutiny than others. Industries that deal with products that impact health and wellness (e.g., food processing firms, tobacco companies, pharmaceutical manufacturers, hospitals and medical centers), that involve public trust (e.g., banking institutions and brokerage houses), and that involve matters of national security (e.g., air carriers) serve as excellent examples of industries that carry increased scrutiny that is due, among other things, to the nature of the goods and services that they provide.

Marketers, of course, must be mindful of the political environment as it ultimately can enhance or constrain sales activities for associated product offerings.

Economic Forces

Economic forces involve all aspects associated with the economy of a society. Economic conditions include a variety of factors related to economic health including inflation, unemployment, and income. The economic climate exerts a powerful influence on both organizations and individuals. In weak economies, business entities might scale back or even eliminate product offerings. Rising costs might deter companies from introducing new products or upgrading technologies. Poor economies might even result in the closure of establishments.

An environment of company layoffs and closures quite obviously has a negative impact on consumer spending. Such an environment can destroy the demand for "want" items, such as luxury automobiles, jewelry, gourmet food, and the like. It can even curtail the demand for "need" items, such as food, water, clothing, medicine, electricity for the home, and so on. Alternatively, strong economies can stimulate consumption of product offerings and positively impact the depth and breadth of goods and services offered by business entities.

Social Forces

The social climate of a society impacts virtually every organization operating within the particular environment. Social forces include

FIGURE 19-1: The PEST Analysis

Political Forces	Economic Forces	Social Forces	Technological Forces
1. _____	1. _____	1. _____	1. _____
2. _____	2. _____	2. _____	2. _____
3. _____	3. _____	3. _____	3. _____
4. _____	4. _____	4. _____	4. _____
5. _____	5. _____	5. _____	5. _____
6. _____	6. _____	6. _____	6. _____
7. _____	7. _____	7. _____	7. _____
8. _____	8. _____	8. _____	8. _____
9. _____	9. _____	9. _____	9. _____
10. _____	10. _____	10. _____	10. _____

such aspects as the demographic composition (e.g., age, gender, race, family size, education) and system of values and beliefs (e.g., altruistic/ selfish, moral/immoral) of a society.

Social forces significantly impact what consumers want and need and, thus, dictate what consumers will and will not purchase. A youthful population, for example, will want and need goods and services that differ from those desired by an aging population, and marketers must be able to deliver accordingly. The same would be true of the prevailing values of consumers in the marketplace. Periods of altruism may likely result in reduced demand for luxury goods if consumer resources are diverted to assist worthy causes.

Regardless of the social forces at play in a given setting, marketers must be prepared to accurately assess prevailing characteristics and target their products in a manner to elicit desired results, namely positive sales growth.

Technological Forces

Technological forces significantly influence broad society in virtually every conceivable manner. Business entities have benefited from technological innovation both internally, by incorporating various advancements into their operations (e.g., wireless communications, e-commerce solutions), and externally, by incorporating the latest technologies into product offerings for sale to customers (e.g., cellular telephones equipped with digital cameras, automobiles equipped with global positioning systems). Innovations are likely to become all the more spectacular with promising new developments in biotechnology, nanotechnology, and other scientific frontiers, which will provide new opportunities for business entities to further realize internal and external gains.

In Practice

Formulating a PEST Analysis requires that marketers (1) construct a PEST diagram such as the one illustrated in Figure 19-1, (2) identify relevant macro-environmental forces, and (3) describe how these forces are expected to impact their specific entities. The resulting diagram is then analyzed to gain macro-environmental insights.

FIGURE 19-2: A Fast Food Restaurant Chain's PEST Analysis

Political Forces	Economic Forces	Social Forces	Technological Forces
Federal lawmakers desire enhanced nutritional information for fast food items ...*expected to*... Increase consumer awareness of nutritional value of fast foods via issuance of new product information guidelines	**Robust economy: rising income, low unemployment** ...*expected to*... Increase customer traffic; reduce availability of fast food labor force	**Growth of dual-career couples with young children** ...*expected to*... Increase demand for meals prepared outside of home	**New drive-thru ordering system** ...*expected to*... Improve communication and increase order accuracy
Court tosses case of individuals charging fast food establishments with damaging their health ...*expected to*... Affirm that personal food consumption decisions rest with individuals; relieve fast food industry of litigation threats	**Significant industrial growth and expansion** ...*expected to*... Increase demand for new restaurants in growing areas	**Adult and child obesity on the rise** ...*expected to*... Increase demand for broad health and fitness initiatives including dietary health programs; increase demand for healthy menu items	**Improved cooking technologies** ...*expected to*... Improve abilities to quickly prepare food **Newly developed environment-friendly food service paper products** ...*expected to*... Reduce environmental contaminants resulting from trash disposal

Figure 19-2 presents a completed PEST Analysis for a fast food restaurant chain which clearly and concisely identifies relevant macro-environmental forces. With this tool, the company can quickly assess macro-environmental influences and formulate strategies and tactics to address pressing issues. Opportunities can be identified and ideally exploited, while threats can be assessed and potentially avoided or eliminated. The PEST Analysis allows organizations to proactively, rather than reactively, address macro-environmental forces.

Importantly, the PEST Analysis should be conducted in an inclusive fashion where input from all organizational members involved in the development and management of associated goods and services is actively encouraged. The multiple perspectives offered by this extended group of individuals can greatly enhance resulting PEST Analyses.

It should be noted that the information derived from the PEST Analysis should ideally be combined with micro-environmental information (e.g., information regarding suppliers, competitors, and customers). When this is accomplished, organizations possess a complete environmental assessment—invaluable information for planning marketing strategies and tactics.

In Summary

With its external focus, the PEST Analysis provides marketers with a useful method for monitoring the macro-environment. By routinely conducting this analysis, marketers can proactively respond to opportunities and threats that exist in the larger environment, allowing their organizations the increased opportunity to achieve growth and prosperity.

THE SWOT ANALYSIS

Progressive marketers routinely engage in the systematic evaluation of their product offerings and associated target markets. To assist marketers in this evaluative process, they often rely on a tool known as the SWOT Analysis. Illustrated in Figure 20-1, the SWOT Analysis involves the identification of institutional strengths, weaknesses, opportunities, and threats. As indicated in the diagram, strengths and weaknesses relate to internal environmental factors, while opportunities and threats pertain to external environmental factors. The SWOT Analysis is also known as a *situation analysis* because it focuses on the state of affairs of an organization.

Although the SWOT Analysis has traditionally been used for institutional assessment purposes, it also serves as a highly effective tool for marketers when the focal point of the analysis is shifted from the organization to its product offerings. Instead of assessing the organization (e.g., Capital Manufacturing), marketers analyze the strengths, weaknesses, opportunities, and threats of associated product offerings (e.g., Capital Manufacturing's lawn mowers, snow blowers, garden tillers, edgers, and chain saws). Strengths, weaknesses, opportunities, and threats are defined as follows:

Strengths

Strengths are positive product and product-related attributes that facilitate exchange. Attributes such as outstanding quality, excellent brand identity, increasing market share, excellent marketing management,

FIGURE 20-1: The SWOT Analysis

	Strengths	Weaknesses
INTERNAL	1. _____ 2. _____ 3. _____ 4. _____ 5. _____	1. _____ 2. _____ 3. _____ 4. _____ 5. _____
	Opportunities	**Threats**
EXTERNAL	1. _____ 2. _____ 3. _____ 4. _____ 5. _____	1. _____ 2. _____ 3. _____ 4. _____ 5. _____

superior research and development, world-class customer service, and patent protection are all examples of product and product-related strengths. Through exploitation of strengths, marketers can make great progress in the realization of marketing goals.

Weaknesses

Weaknesses are negative product and product-related attributes that adversely impact exchange. Weaknesses might include poor customer service, inconvenient access to offerings, inferior product quality, outdated technology, decreasing market share, inadequate advertising funds, and so on. Weaknesses undermine product performance and, ultimately, exchange in the marketplace. Therefore, positive steps must be taken to eliminate these negative attributes.

Opportunities

Opportunities are external events and circumstances that have the potential to positively impact products. Opportunities might include newly discovered product uses, increasing market growth, newly developed technologies, anticipated favorable government legislation, and so on. Marketers must vigorously pursue and capitalize on opportunities in order to increase the likelihood of institutional survival, growth, and prosperity.

Threats

Threats are external events and circumstances that have the potential to negatively impact products. Threats might include declining market growth, new competitors, anticipated adverse government legislation, changing customer preferences, competitors equipped with superior technologies, and superior substitute products. Marketers must endeavor to develop strategies and tactics that will reduce or eliminate the potentially detrimental impact of threats.

In Practice

Formulating a SWOT Analysis requires that marketers (1) construct a SWOT diagram such as the one illustrated in Figure 20-1, (2) determine the particular product that will be evaluated, and (3) identify associated strengths, weaknesses, opportunities, and threats. The resulting diagram is then analyzed to gain product insights.

Figure 20-2 presents a completed SWOT Analysis for an appliance manufacturer's television sets. This diagram illustrates the concise information portrayal offered by this simple, yet highly effective, marketing tool. With this tool, marketers can quickly assess internal and external product and product-related characteristics and influences—information that is essential for monitoring current performance and determining future strategic and tactical pursuits.

The SWOT Analysis can be used not only to assess the products held by entities, but also to analyze the offerings of competitors. This method simply requires that marketers gain information regarding competitive offerings and then perform related SWOT Analyses. By using the SWOT Analysis in this fashion, many useful insights can be gained which can assist marketers in formulating marketing strategies and tactics.

Although marketers will be most concerned with the strengths, weaknesses, opportunities, and threats associated with the products they are responsible for managing, they must not neglect the value of performing the traditional, organization-focused SWOT Analysis. Goods and services are products of the organizations that produce and provide them. Coupling product-focused SWOT Analyses with organization-focused assessments will undoubtedly provide a higher degree of insight into marketing operations.

It should be noted that while multiple SWOT Analyses are virtually required for organizations with multiple product offerings, such detail may not be necessary in organizations with very few products. A small, independent coffee shop, for example, would likely require only one SWOT Analysis. Here, the organization and its product offerings are

FIGURE 20-2: An Appliance Company's SWOT Analysis (TVs)

	Strengths	Weaknesses
INTERNAL	Newly constructed manufacturing plant Greater capacity than competitors Best technology in the industry Most reputable product engineers Longest warranty in the industry Large advertising budget	Product features not as elaborate as competitors Inadequate product support compared to competitors High assembly line employee turnover
	Opportunities	**Threats**
EXTERNAL	Increasing interest in home entertainment Possible closure of one competing manufacturer New and improved technologies available soon	Seven competing manufacturers One new competitor expected in 6 months Parts shortages expected over next 3 months Increasing fuel prices driving up product shipping costs

virtually one in the same. A single SWOT Analysis would, therefore, be sufficient.

Importantly, the SWOT Analysis should be conducted in an inclusive fashion where input from all organizational members involved in the development and management of associated goods and services is actively encouraged. The multiple perspectives offered by this extended group of individuals can greatly enhance resulting SWOT Analyses.

In Summary

The SWOT Analysis provides a simple, convenient, and effective method for quickly assessing the internal and external factors associated with products and the organizations that produce and provide them. Knowledge of this information allows marketers to formulate success-generating strategies and tactics that will yield positive marketing outcomes.

MICHAEL PORTER'S FIVE FORCES MODEL

21

The marketplace is characterized by intense competition and rivalry, elements that will only intensify as business entities of all kinds vie for the opportunity to serve target markets. Those entities that can successfully navigate the complex business environment will be handsomely rewarded with increased market share and prosperity.

Successful navigation of this environment, of course, requires a deep understanding of marketplace competitors. All too often, however, entities view their competitive environment in an overly narrow fashion that fails to acknowledge the true depth and breadth of competitive forces in the marketplace. Competition is multidimensional and its vastness must be clearly understood if marketing success is to be achieved. The critical task of accurately identifying the competitive elements in a market is greatly facilitated by Michael Porter's Five Forces Model.

Illustrated in Figure 21-1, Porter's Five Forces Model provides useful insights into the multifaceted nature of competition. According to Porter, the nature of competition in an industry is based on five forces: existing competitors, potential entrants, substitutes, suppliers, and buyers.

These forces are unique to each industry (and industry segment) and combine to determine the competitive intensity and ultimate potential of associated markets. These five forces are explained as follows:

Existing Competitors

Existing competitors are the most obvious competitive force, jockeying for position through new product development, innovative promotional campaigns, and the like. Rivalry among existing competitors is especially intense when competitors are numerous and fairly equivalent in terms of size and power, when exit barriers are high, and when industry growth is slow resulting in struggles for market share. These characteristics are frequently observed across all industries, illustrating the intense rivalry within the marketplace.

Potential Entrants

Entities that might potentially enter the market represent significant threats to existing competitors. New entrants bring new capacity and resources to the market, along with desires for market share. The magnitude of the threat posed by new entrants is largely based on the particular barriers to entry that exist.

Typical examples of entry barriers include capital requirements, proprietary product differences, government policy, and the market dominance and brand identity of existing competitors. Significant entry barriers yield significant protection from the threat of new entrants, while few barriers increase the competitive nature of the market.

Substitutes

Substitutes are products that differ from particular offerings but largely, and sometimes completely, fill equivalent wants and needs. As a result, substitute offerings can greatly affect the performance of business entities and even their very existence.

Bottled water, for example, could be viewed as a substitute for soft drinks. Poultry could be viewed as a substitute for beef. Cellular telephone service could be viewed as a substitute for landline telephone service. Air transportation could be viewed as a substitute for rail transportation.

The seriousness of the threat of substitutes is predominantly based on their performance and price characteristics. Substitutes that offer equal or better performance pose significant threats, especially when price advantages exist.

Suppliers

Suppliers provide the components necessary for business entities to offer goods and services to their customers. Restaurants, for example, require food products, utensils, cooking equipment, and so on. Shipping companies require cargo vans and aircraft, forklifts, containers and pallets, transit information systems, etc. Automobile manufacturers require steel, glass, plastics, engines, tires, and so forth. Without these "raw materials," entities could not function. This dependence on suppliers poses a significant threat to business establishments.

FIGURE 21-1: Porter's Five Forces Model

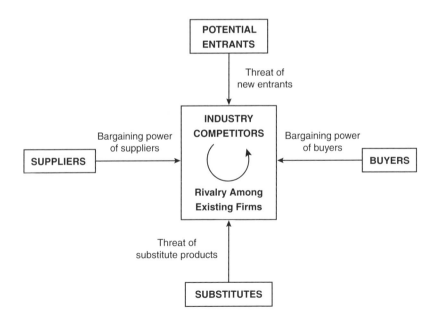

FIGURE 21-2: A Five Forces Worksheet

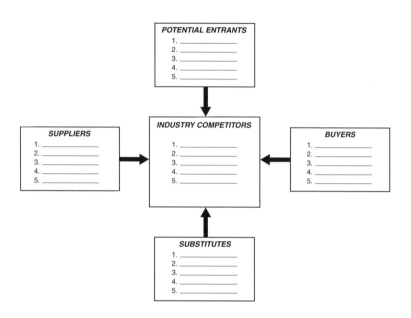

Suppliers can raise their prices, lower the quality of the components that they provide, or simply go out of business—all situations that can yield potentially devastating effects. Suppliers are particularly powerful if they are few in number, if few substitutes exist, and if entities are not key customers.

Buyers

Porter's term "buyers" is equivalent to the term "customers," which is better suited for many industries. Quite obviously, customers possess significant bargaining power over business entities because their patronage ultimately determines institutional survival, growth, and prosperity. Without customers, operations cease. For this reason, marketers must ensure that all marketing efforts are customer-focused. Importantly, marketers must strive to accurately assess the wants and needs of customers and serve them in a manner that will meet and exceed their expectations.

In Practice

Porter's Five Forces Model is highly useful in that it clearly illustrates the multidimensional nature of marketplace competition. Its use, however, can greatly be extended through the assembly and completion of a Five Forces Worksheet. Marketers simply (1) identify the product offering to be evaluated, (2) construct the Five Forces Worksheet as illustrated in Figure 21-2, (3) identify existing competitors, potential entrants, substitutes, suppliers, and buyers, and (4) place the identified current and potential competitors on the worksheet accordingly. Once

FIGURE 21-3: A Restaurant's Five Forces Worksheet

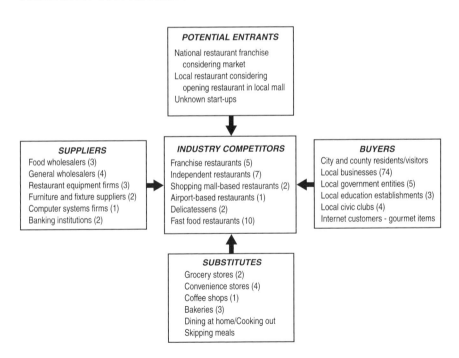

completed, the Five Forces Worksheet clearly identifies all five competitive forces that entities currently face or could potentially face, as illustrated in Figure 21-3. Completion of this simple, yet highly effective, worksheet yields considerable insights into the current and future competitive marketplace and, hence, serves as an essential marketing planning tool.

In Summary

By clearly illustrating the true depth and breadth of the competitive environment, Porter's Five Forces Model serves as an indispensable resource for marketers. With this information, marketers can establish strategic and tactical priorities and position their organizations to capitalize on opportunities and avoid or eliminate threats. Ideally, marketers will address each of the five forces. By properly addressing the complete competitive environment, marketers are better prepared to meet and exceed market share and related performance objectives.

REFERENCE:

Porter, Michael E. *Competitive Strategy: Techniques for Analyzing Industries and Competitors.* New York: The Free Press, 1998.

THE LEHMANN & WINER
LEVELS OF COMPETITION MODEL

22

Progressive marketers understand that it is essential to accurately identify and assess their competition, as every competitor represents a threat. Although marketers cannot control their competitors, they can closely monitor the actions of rivals and proactively address developing issues.

When marketers fail to identify competitors, they inadvertently afford the unidentified rivals with the strategic advantage of operational secrecy. This gives competitors the element of surprise and, along with it, valuable time to secure market share.

Possibly the most common competitive assessment error committed by marketers is that of defining the competitive field too narrowly. To assist marketers in understanding the true extent of the competitive environment, Donald Lehmann and Russell Winer developed a diagram that depicts levels of market competition.

Illustrated in Figure 22-1, the Lehmann and Winer Levels of Competition Model identifies four competitive levels (product form, product category, generic, and budget) that are depicted by four concentric circles which surround the product under evaluation. Competitive offerings are placed on this diagram based on how they compare to the product under evaluation. Competitive products occupying inner levels of the diagram are more comparable to the product under evaluation than those occupying outer levels. The four competitive levels are defined as follows:

Product Form Competition

Product form competition is the narrowest view that can be taken of competition. Identified by the innermost circle on the Levels of Competition Model, product form competition includes all competitive products that have roughly equivalent product features and compete in the same market segments. At this level, competitive entities include those direct, head-to-head rivals that offer similar goods and services and compete for the same "turf."

Product Category Competition

The level just beyond product form competition is known as product category competition. Here, competition expands to include all com-

---

FIGURE 22-1: The Lehmann & Winer Levels of Competition Model

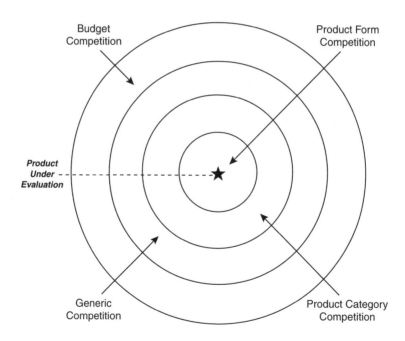

Adapted from *Analysis for Marketing Planning*, 5th ed. by Donald R. Lehmann and Russell S. Winer. Copyright © 2002, 1997, 1994, 1991, 1988 by The McGraw-Hill Companies, Inc. Published by McGraw-Hill. Reproduced with permission of The McGraw-Hill Companies.

petitive products that possess similar features, regardless of the market segments targeted. Competition at this level represents what marketing managers have traditionally viewed as their competitive set.

Generic Competition

The third level of competition is known as generic competition. Generic competition includes all competing products that, although unrelated to given product offerings, fill equivalent wants and needs. Whereas product form and product category levels are inward-focused (focused on products similar to those produced and provided by given entities), generic competition is outward-focused (focused on potential alternatives or substitutes for associated product offerings). Marketers wishing to capitalize on opportunities and avoid threats must be certain that their view of competition includes the generic level. Such a focus will ensure that marketers avoid what Theodore Levitt termed *marketing myopia* in his classic 1960 article of the same title, a detrimental practice where entities define their businesses too narrowly.

Budget Competition

Budget competition, the outermost level of competition, involves all products that compete for the same customer dollar. Budget competition represents the broadest view of competition. Although budget competition is useful from a conceptual perspective, it is of very little strategic value because the number of potential competitive offerings is so immense.

In Practice

To assess product competition using the Lehmann and Winer Levels of Competition Model, marketers simply (1) identify the product offering to be evaluated, (2) construct the Levels of Competition diagram as illustrated in Figure 22-1, (3) identify product form, product category, generic, and budget competitors, and (4) place the identified competitors on the diagram accordingly. The resulting Levels of Competition diagram is then analyzed to gain insights into product competition.

Figure 22-2 presents a Levels of Competition Model that was developed for an urban medical center that primarily serves an affluent, privately insured customer population. At the product form level, the medical center would view its competition as other area medical centers that provide the same services to the same affluent, insured customer population. The product category level represents a broadened competitive scope that would include all medical centers in the marketplace, regardless of the clientele served. Here, the medical center

---

FIGURE 22-2: A Medical Center's Levels of Competition Model

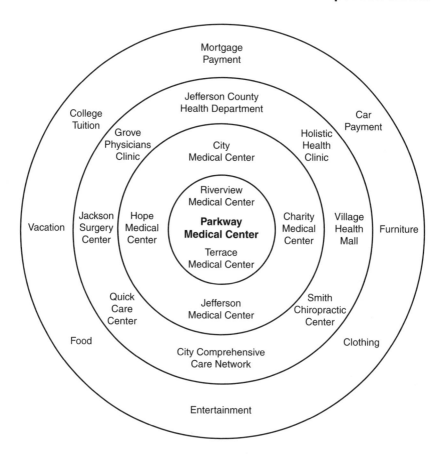

Adapted from *Analysis for Marketing Planning*, 5th ed. by Donald R. Lehmann and Russell S. Winer. Copyright © 2002, 1997, 1994, 1991, 1988 by The McGraw-Hill Companies, Inc. Published by McGraw-Hill. Reproduced with permission of The McGraw-Hill Companies.

would include facilities that serve low-income customers, along with all other medical centers in the marketplace, regardless of the particular target markets.

At the generic level, the competitive scope increases significantly to include facilities that address similar wants and needs. Here, the medical center would add area clinics, health departments, and other health service providers to its competitive framework. Although these entities

FIGURE 22-3: A Golf Course's Levels of Competition Model

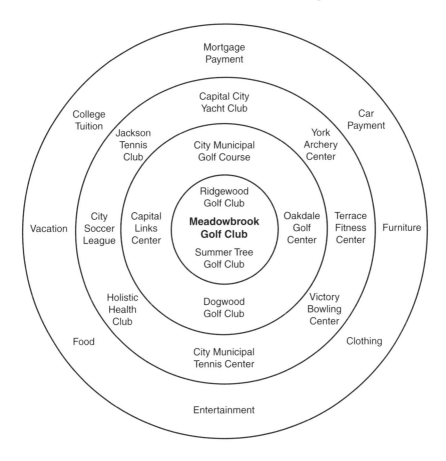

do not directly compete with the medical center, they do offer alternatives in many clinical areas for prospective customers.

Lastly, budget competition could be anything and everything, health-care-related or not, that might divert customer resources away from the medical center. An individual might, for example, forgo an elective medical procedure (or even one that is medically necessary!) to pay for his or her child's college tuition, to take a vacation, to buy a new car, to purchase furniture, etc.

Figure 22-3 presents a Levels of Competition Model that was developed for a private golf course providing recreation to a members-only customer population. At the product form level, the golf course would view its competition as other area golf courses that provide the same services to the same customer population. The product category level represents a broadened competitive scope that would include all golf courses in the marketplace, regardless of the population served. Here, the golf course would add area golf courses that are open to the public.

At the generic level, the competitive scope increases to include sports and recreation entities that address similar wants and needs, namely the enjoyment of fitness-related activities. Here, the golf course would add area tennis clubs, yacht clubs, fitness centers, and other sports and recreation service providers to its competitive framework. All of these entities provide sports and recreation alternatives for prospective customers. Lastly, budget competition would include anything that would compete for the golf recreation dollars of customers—a down payment on a house, a computer, clothing, jewelry, etc.

It is important to note that the Levels of Competition Model does not assess the threat potential forwarded by competitive elements. For example, in Figure 22-3, it might be very likely that a generic competitor, such as a yacht club, might pose more of a threat to the private golf course under evaluation than a product category competitor, such as a public golf course. The model instead identifies competitive elements based on their characteristics in relation to the product under evaluation. It categorizes competition by "type" of competitor, which does not necessarily equate with threat intensity.

Given this, it might be useful to indicate on the Levels of Competition diagram those offerings, regardless of their competitive level, that are believed to pose the most significant threat to the product under evaluation. This kind of information greatly assists marketers in determining strategic and tactical priorities, particularly in the area of product promotion.

In Summary

Given the dangers associated with defining the competitive field too narrowly, marketers must diligently seek to identify all current and potential rivals in the market. The Lehmann and Winer Levels of Competition Model serves as a useful guide for marketers to consult in this pursuit, reminding them of the true extent of competitive elements in the marketplace.

REFERENCES:

Lehmann, Donald R., and Russell S. Winer. *Analysis for Marketing Planning.* 5th ed. New York: McGraw-Hill, 2002.

Levitt, Theodore. "Marketing Myopia." *Harvard Business Review* (July-August) 1960: 45-56.

THE MINTZBERG & VAN DER HEYDEN ORGANIGRAPH

Progressive marketers understand that, in order to achieve marketing success, they must possess a deep understanding of their organizations, the products offered, the markets sought, and associated environmental relationships. With such knowledge, marketers are able to formulate productive strategies that yield positive marketing results.

Gaining this extensive insight into inter- and intraorganizational relationships, however, is not a simple activity as these facets are normally quite complex. Achieving this understanding can be hastened, however, by assembling and analyzing an Organigraph, a useful tool developed by Henry Mintzberg and Ludo Van der Heyden.

In essence, the Organigraph is a diagram that depicts the activities and operations of organizations. Mintzberg and Van der Heyden developed the Organigraph to shed light on the often complex inter- and intraorganizational relationships of institutions—a feat that the traditional organizational chart cannot accomplish. The authors named their new tool after the word *organigramme*, the French term for organizational chart.

Rather than using the series of boxes and lines that are common in organizational charts, the Organigraph uses a series of shapes to illustrate the actual relationships that exist inside and outside of organizations. This feature greatly increases the level of detail that can be incorporated into these diagrams.

Although the construction and use of Organigraphs is typically associated with strategic management, these tools also have marketing applications. By depicting inter- and intraorganizational relationships, most notably those dealing with suppliers and target markets, Organigraphs can be quite helpful to marketers seeking an overall view of their entities and associated interrelationships, many of which directly impact marketing.

Constructing an Organigraph

Constructing an Organigraph requires imagination. Unlike organizational charts which have strict rules governing their assembly, Organi-

---

FIGURE 23-1: Common Components of Organigraphs

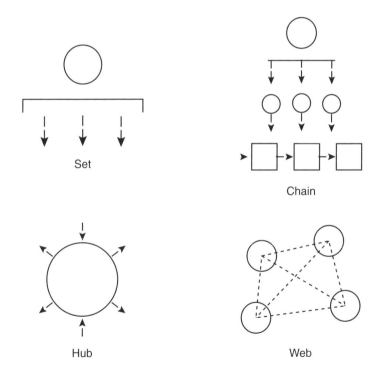

Set

Chain

Hub

Web

graphs do not possess such guidelines. Marketers are simply required to (1) think about their organizations, the products offered, the markets sought, and associated environmental relationships and (2) map this vision using a series of shapes that accurately illustrates associated activities and operations.

As illustrated in Figure 23-1, Organigraphs are typically assembled using some combination of four primary components: sets, chains, hubs, and webs. A set indicates an independent relationship; a chain indicates the progressive development or assembly of something; a hub indicates a coordinating center that links activities; and a web indicates a series of "nodes" depicting relationships among components that do not possess a coordinating center. Other shapes can, of course, be used to assemble Organigraphs, provided that the shapes accurately convey relationships.

In Practice

Figure 23-2 illustrates an Organigraph that was constructed for a shopping arcade. Quite noticeably, the Organigraph is shaped as a "web," indicating the presence of relationships among the shopping arcade's four tenants: Capital City Tailor, Capital City Cobbler, Capital City Coffee Shop, and Capital City Barber Shop.

As indicated in the diagram, each of these tenants interacts with one another but operates in a largely autonomous fashion. These stores, for example, independently serve customers, coordinate internal activities, and manage customer account information. Also of note in the Organigraph is the depiction of the shopping establishment's customer base, identified by customer type and geographic location. If desired, the shopping arcade could create a more detailed Organigraph that illustrates suppliers, competitors, and so on. With this additional detail, the Organigraph easily becomes a strategic tool that possesses value for all tenants within the shopping establishment.

Figure 23-3 depicts an Organigraph that was developed for a furniture manufacturer. This diagram clearly illustrates the central coordinat-

FIGURE 23-2: A Shopping Arcade's Organigraph

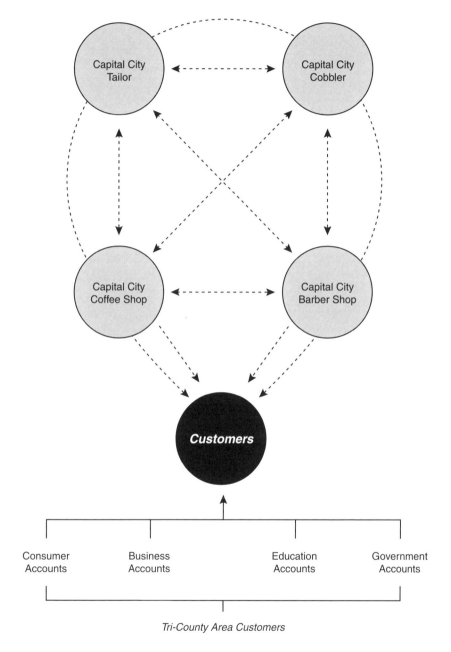

Tri-County Area Customers

Constructed using design methodology in "Organigraphs: Drawing How Companies Really Work" by Henry Mintzberg and Ludo Van der Heyden. *Harvard Business Review* (September-October) 1999: 87-94.

FIGURE 23-3: A Furniture Manufacturer's Organigraph

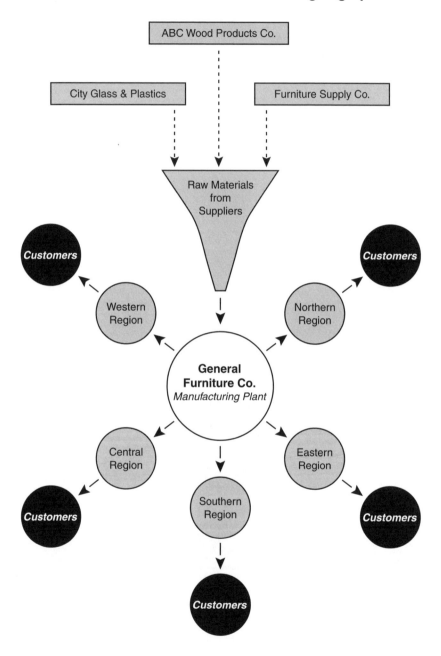

Constructed using design methodology in "Organigraphs: Drawing How Companies Really Work" by Henry Mintzberg and Ludo Van der Heyden. *Harvard Business Review* (September-October) 1999: 87-94.

ing role of the entity's manufacturing plant (as depicted by its "hub" shape) which constructs furniture products and distributes items to five regional showrooms which are ultimately responsible for delivering furniture products to customers. In illustrating the supplier role in this diagram, the manufacturer uses a "funnel" shape to indicate the collection of multiple elements (raw materials from suppliers) that are directed in a coordinated fashion into the manufacturing plant for use in the furniture production process. If desired, of course, more detail could be added to the diagram, increasing its value and use within the furniture manufacturing company.

In Summary

The Mintzberg and Van der Heyden Organigraph provides marketers with a powerful tool for achieving a thorough understanding of their organizations, the products offered, the markets sought, and associated environmental relationships. The diagram's flexibility allows marketers to illustrate virtually any institutional relationship. By understanding the many inter- and intraorganizational relationships of entities, marketers are better prepared to develop appropriate, success-generating marketing strategies.

REFERENCE:

Mintzberg, Henry, and Ludo Van der Heyden. "Organigraphs: Drawing How Companies Really Work." *Harvard Business Review* (September-October) 1999: 87-94.

PART FIVE

MARKETING STRATEGY
&
PLANNING TOOLS

24

Leonard Berry's Success Sustainability Model

Administrative excellence does not arise out of luck or chance, but rather through the development and implementation of appropriate institutional systems that guide entities to prosperity. Numerous systems must be incorporated but possibly none is as important as the underlying array of principles embraced by business entities. The composition of these principles ultimately determines the potential of organizations to achieve and sustain success.

To understand the prerequisites for sustained operational excellence, marketers often refer to Leonard Berry's Success Sustainability Model, which was developed from Berry's research inquiries into the practices of top-performing service organizations.

Illustrated in Figure 24-1, Berry's Success Sustainability Model is depicted as a circular diagram containing nine boxes that denote "drivers" of excellence. Eight of these drivers (strategic focus, executional excellence, control of destiny, trust-based relationships, investment in employee success, acting small, brand cultivation, and generosity) occupy boxes that encompass the perimeter of the diagram, each extending from the primary driver (values-driven leadership) situated in the center of the diagram.

Arrows drawn with solid lines denote primary relationships, while those drawn with dotted lines indicate interrelationships among success drivers. The nine drivers of excellence are defined as follows:

Values-Driven Leadership

Values-driven leadership serves as the foundation or root of all other drivers of excellence. Values represent the core beliefs held by business entities. If these values are not strong, sustainable success cannot be achieved. Importantly, entities seeking sustained success must possess seven core values, namely excellence (striving for high performance in all areas), innovation (striving to make current offerings better), joy (working to uplift the human spirit and celebrate achievement), teamwork (collaborating to achieve common goals), respect (concern for employees, customers, suppliers, etc.), integrity (conducting operations in an ethical fashion), and social profit (giving back to the community).

These values must actively be communicated by leaders, demonstrated through value-laden actions, and cultivated in order to achieve excellence. By embracing these values, business entities establish solid institutional foundations that foster excellence.

Strategic Focus

Organizations seeking sustained success must formulate strategies that embody their embraced values. This specifically requires that entities clearly define their businesses and develop specialized systems of activities to implement their missions. Strategies should reflect the dynamic and innovative nature of entities. Importantly, business establishments must strive to ensure that their strategies remain mission-focused, as deviations hamper the attainment of excellence.

A department store that, for example, embraces a mission of providing comprehensive retail services to rural populations must formulate an array of strategies that focuses exclusively on the delivery of quality retail services to its rural target market. If the entity deviates from its mission by formulating divergent strategies that target, say, urban populations, the retailer has obviously lost sight of its mission and will ultimately suffer the perils associated with a failed strategic focus, notably institutional decline and possibly failure.

Executional Excellence

Not only must business entities formulate well-planned strategies, but they also must ensure that these strategies are appropriately and successfully executed through sound tactics. Execution is as important as the strategy itself and progressive entities place a significant emphasis on excellence in this area. Tactical pursuits must flow directly from the strategies embraced by entities in order for excellence to be achieved. Through well-executed tactics, strategic goals and objectives are accom-

FIGURE 24-1: Berry's Success Sustainability Model

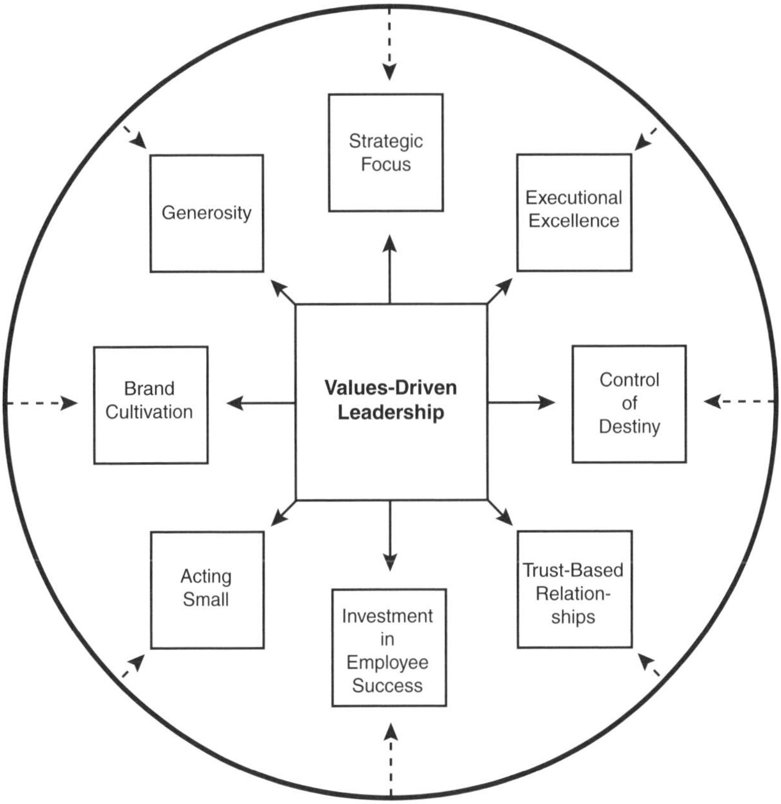

plished, thus fulfilling associated missions. The best developed missions and accompanying strategies are pointless if they are not executed appropriately through sound tactics, hence the importance of excellence in this area.

Control of Destiny

Control of destiny is largely an attitudinal mindset which holds that, by taking appropriate actions, business entities can control the future. Such actions taken by business entities in an effort to control their destiny might include the continuous enhancement of institutional technologies, the recruitment and retention of highly skilled employees, the delivery of products that possess greater value than competitive offerings, and the establishment of world-class customer service.

Entities that possess a control of destiny mindset are prepared to positively address the rigorous business environment and its associated challenges. This positive mindset undoubtedly motivates establishments to take success-generating actions that enhance prosperity.

Trust-Based Relationships

Organizations cannot attain success without conducting all operations in a genuine fashion. This involves honoring obligations and commitments, treating all parties fairly and respectfully, maintaining confidentiality, and so on. When a bank takes steps to ensure that its tellers address bank patrons in a timely and courteous manner, it establishes trust with its clients. When an automobile manufacturer incorporates the latest technologies into its automobiles, it establishes trust with the customers that it serves.

When a department store meets financial obligations with its vendors in a timely fashion, it establishes trust with these various suppliers. When a medical center ensures that patient confidentiality is maintained, it establishes trust with its patient population. Trust allows the formation of lasting, commitment-laden relationships with customers, employees, suppliers, and communities.

Investment in Employee Success

A talented labor force represents a key source of competitive advantage. The ability to recruit and retain the best employees requires an investment in their professional growth and development that indirectly represents an investment in the establishments sponsoring such assistance. The marketplace is continuously changing and business entities must ensure that their employees possess the tools necessary for enduring success.

Mechanisms for providing such tools include funding continuing education coursework, sponsoring college tuition reimbursement programs, and providing on-site educational seminars for personnel. Employees receiving such institutional assistance will have both the ability and the desire to return the investment through service excellence.

Acting Small

Large and small organizations each possess advantages and disadvantages associated with scale. Large entities have the luxury of economies of scale, more notoriety, and a larger customer base. Smaller entities, however, possess their share of advantages, too. These include nimbleness, less bureaucracy, and more personal, customized service.

Given the ever-changing nature of the marketplace, coupled with increasing customer demands for personal service and attention, organizations would do well to remember the positive attributes associated with small entities and ensure that these characteristics are incorporated into their operations.

Brand Cultivation

Through branding, business entities give their products *identity*. Brand identity greatly assists customers in the process of product differentiation and, therefore, represents a key source of competitive advantage. Upstanding organizations that successfully brand themselves and their products afford customers with assurances of quality that facilitate lasting patronage. Given the importance of branding, entities must strive to develop (cultivate) their brands in an effort to capitalize on the many associated benefits.

In some situations, particular business entities represent, in and of themselves, the brands to be cultivated. In other situations, units within business establishments may each represent brands to be cultivated. A large shipping company, for example, might seek to brand its multiple divisions (e.g., ground, air, freight), as well as itself. Similarly, goods-producing firms, like computer manufacturers, often brand individual products, as well as themselves, in an effort to capitalize on the benefits of branding.

Generosity

Institutional generosity acts as a catalyst to all things good within organizations and even beyond. Acts of kindness, such as sponsoring student education programs, awarding scholarships to members of the community, and supporting charitable foundations inspire customers, employees, suppliers, and communities. Through generosity, business entities become more than producers and providers of products; they become true members of the greater community—an appropriate place for any establishment.

In Practice

Clearly, business entities that incorporate the nine drivers of excellence identified by Berry are well on their way to achieving success in the marketplace. All too often, however, the change-rich environment of the marketplace directs attention away from these important drivers of sustainable success, which is the reason many business entities fail to meet and exceed the expectations of their target markets. Ensuring the presence of these drivers does indeed require significant effort. Those establishments that are willing to incorporate the success drivers into their daily operations position themselves for enduring growth and prosperity.

In Summary

Berry's Success Sustainability Model clearly illustrates the drivers of excellence that business entities must possess if they desire sustained growth and prosperity. Given the competitive nature of the market-place along with its environmental complexities, business entities would do well to incorporate the nine drivers of excellence into their operations in order to reap the many benefits of sustained success.

REFERENCE:

Berry, Leonard L. *Discovering the Soul of Service: The Nine Drivers of Sustainable Business Success*. New York: The Free Press, 1999.

25

GEORGE DAY'S
MARKET ORIENTATION MODEL

Progressive marketers understand that marketing success is largely based on how well they assess and address the markets they serve. This requires, among other things, the accurate assessment of customer wants and needs, the provision of products that effectively address those wants and needs, and the proactive assessment and management of competitive threats in the environment. Simply stated, these marketers understand the importance of being market-driven.

When marketers adopt a market-driven mindset, they are perfectly positioned to capitalize on opportunities and avoid or eliminate threats in the environment. Through this proactive, externally-focused stance, marketers are able to thoroughly understand their target markets and deliver product solutions that will earn confidence and trust, ultimately resulting in the ongoing, valuable patronage of customers.

Despite the benefits associated with being market-driven, many marketers fail to successfully incorporate this mindset, largely because of institutional systems that support inside-out, rather than outside-in, approaches. Organizations embracing such inside-out approaches allow internal factors such as prior histories and traditions, existing internal capabilities, and so on to guide operational decisions rather than the externally-based wants and needs of target markets. Only by being market-driven, an outside-in approach, can establishments deliver superior customer value and reap the many benefits associated with this philosophy.

Organizations seeking to become market-driven must shift their focus to the market. To assist entities in this transformation, George Day developed the Market Orientation Model, a diagram that presents the components of a market-driven organization. Illustrated in Figure 25-1, Day's Market Orientation Model consists of an oval, representing the internal environment of an organization, which encompasses a series of four circles, representing the entity's shared knowledge base and the three elements of a market orientation: culture, capabilities, and configuration. These three elements are defined as follows:

Culture

Culture, specifically one that is externally-oriented, represents the first element of Day's Market Orientation Model. Culture can broadly be

FIGURE 25-1: Day's Market Orientation Model

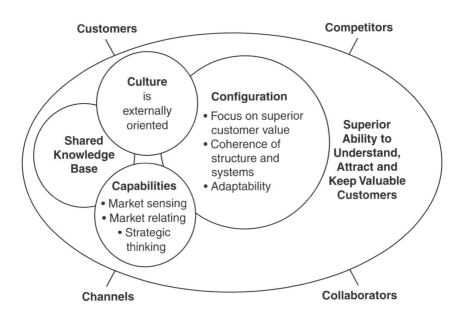

defined as the group of values, beliefs, and behaviors embraced by an organization. Every organization possesses a culture that is unique to that particular entity. Depending on the composition of values, beliefs, and behaviors embraced, culture can positively or negatively influence operations and, once established, culture can be very difficult to change. Market-driven organizations must possess an externally-oriented, participative culture that heavily emphasizes the delivery of superior customer value and continually strives to secure new sources of competitive advantage.

A bank, for example, that seeks to establish an externally-oriented culture must ensure that the appropriate constructs are in place to allow the culture to develop. One such construct is the bank's mission statement. As an openly circulated document, the mission statement is available for internal parties (e.g., executives, officers, tellers), as well as external parties (e.g., stockholders, stakeholders, customers, suppliers), to view and quickly understand the institution's purpose.

When used appropriately, the mission statement serves as a guide for executives and employees to follow in their many operational pursuits. It, therefore, is an excellent starting point for building an externally-oriented culture. Bank officials would simply (1) develop a mission statement that incorporates the elements of an externally-oriented culture (an external, participative orientation emphasizing customer value and the continual search for competitive advantage) and (2) take steps to ensure that they, along with other institutional members, base their actions on this statement. Such a mission statement greatly facilitates the establishment of an externally-oriented culture.

Capabilities

Capabilities represents the second element of Day's Market Orientation Model. Specifically, market-driven organizations must possess distinctive capabilities in the areas of market sensing (the ability to accurately assess and understand markets), market relating (the ability to create and maintain relationships with customers), and strategic thinking (the ability to devise successful strategies that proactively, rather than reactively, address marketplace opportunities and threats). With this set of capabilities, marketers are able to gain a thorough understanding of the customers and markets they serve. They also are able to strategically address associated environmental issues.

The necessity for having these capabilities is all the more essential in today's marketplace, which is characterized by innovation, intense competition, and uncertainty. Given this turbulent environment, marketers must ensure that they acquire and develop market sensing, market relating, and strategic thinking capabilities as they are ultimately the individuals looked to by others in their organizations to provide guidance in environmental assessment and strategic action.

Configuration

Configuration represents the third and final element of Day's Market Orientation Model. This specifically involves the establishment of an organization-wide structure that allows all units within entities to proactively address changing customer requirements and marketplace conditions. In keeping with the attributes associated with market-driven organizations, the particular configuration must emphasize the delivery of superior customer value, incorporate coherence between institutional structures and systems, and be adaptable in order to meet environmental challenges.

The configuration element of Day's Market Orientation Model essentially involves the creation of an institution-wide environment that fosters the development of a market orientation within every departmental unit. This is most beneficial for highly complex establishments which could never hope to be market-driven without creating a configuration that fosters such a mindset across all organizational units.

In Practice

It is important to understand that, in order to be market-driven, the three elements of culture, capabilities, and configuration must be supported by a shared knowledge base. This essentially requires that entities ensure that information is openly shared interorganizationally in an effort to improve overall institutional performance.

All too often, information is poorly disseminated within business entities. This is caused by a variety of factors including poor communications systems, interorganizational conflict, and so on. Regardless of the reasons for poor information dissemination, organizations must take steps to open communications channels so that information can freely flow throughout entities, providing the requisite shared knowledge base that supports the three elements of culture, capabilities, and configuration.

In Summary

Day's Market Orientation Model provides guidance in the assembly of work environments that are externally, rather than internally, focused. By incorporating this orientation, marketers and their organizations become market-driven and are perfectly positioned to capitalize on opportunities and avoid or eliminate threats in the environment, increasing the likelihood of successful commercial endeavors.

REFERENCE:

Day, George S. *The Market Driven Organization: Understanding, Attracting, and Keeping Valuable Customers.* New York: The Free Press, 1999.

MICHAEL PORTER'S VALUE CHAIN

26

The term *competitive advantage* refers to anything possessed by an organization that gives it an edge over its competitors. One key source of competitive advantage is value. Customers seek and base their purchase decisions on value and those entities that can deliver it will be rewarded.

Given the importance of value, its meaning to customers, and its ability to create a competitive advantage, marketers must possess a detailed understanding of this concept and the methods through which value is created—a task greatly facilitated by Michael Porter's Value Chain.

Illustrated in Figure 26-1, Porter's Value Chain is depicted as an arrow-shaped diagram that identifies value-producing activities that are common to all organizations. These value-producing activities are divided into two groups: primary activities (inbound logistics, operations, outbound logistics, marketing and sales, and service) and support activities (firm infrastructure, human resource management, technology development, and procurement).

Each of these activities represents a building block of value and has associated costs. The difference between the total value produced and the collective costs of performing value activities represents the available margin, which varies depending on the skills demonstrated by entities at performing value activities. Primary and support activities are described as follows:

Primary Activities

Primary activities consist of those pursuits that *directly* contribute to the production of specific goods and services. There are five primary activities that are common to all entities: inbound logistics, operations, outbound logistics, marketing and sales, and service. These five activities are identified as follows:

Inbound Logistics

Inbound logistics activities involve all pursuits associated with the management of raw materials necessary to produce goods and services. Typical inbound logistics concerns include materials delivery, materials handling, inventory control, and warehousing. Goods-producing firms like food processing companies, for example, must coordinate deliveries of raw materials (e.g., beef, poultry, spices, flour, sugar) in order to produce their various food offerings. Service-producing firms like hotels and motels, too, must coordinate deliveries of raw materials including furniture and bedding, toiletries, food products, cleaning equipment and supplies, and so on in order to serve guests. Not only must entities secure these products, but they also must effectively manage them through appropriate inventory control systems and warehousing techniques.

Operations

Operations activities involve all pursuits associated with the development and assembly of the goods and services that are to be offered to target markets. Goods-producing firms, such as computer manufacturers and sports equipment production entities, must assemble, test, and package their products. Likewise, apparel manufacturers must produce their various garments and package these goods. Service-producing entities, such as dry cleaning establishments, movie theaters, and automotive repair shops, must assemble and maintain equipment, fixtures, and other service implements and ensure that their facilities are organized for effective service delivery. Operations activities essentially ready products for future purchase and consumption by customers.

Outbound Logistics

Outbound logistics activities involve all pursuits associated with making goods and services available to customers. Tire companies, appliance manufacturers, software companies, and other goods-producing firms must, for example, determine inventory levels, warehouse finished goods, identify distribution channels, and coordinate product deliveries to distributors.

As for service-producing entities, banks, for example, must determine hours of operation and coordinate the schedules of officers and other staff members accordingly. Airlines, rail systems, and bus lines must determine consumer and corporate travel patterns, design applicable schedules, and assemble resources for service delivery. Shipping firms must determine appropriate geographic service delivery areas and coordinate the schedules of delivery personnel. Each of these activities focuses on making product offerings readily available to customers for purchase and consumption.

FIGURE 26-1: Porter's Value Chain

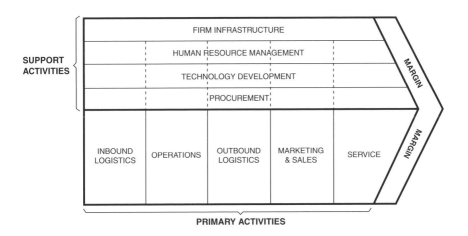

Marketing & Sales

Marketing and sales activities involve all pursuits associated with encouraging customers to purchase and consume product offerings. Such activities include pricing products and promoting these offerings through advertising, personal selling, sales promotion, and other means. Ultimately, these activities seek to encourage exchange between entities and their target markets.

Service

Service activities involve those pursuits that support post-purchase/post-consumption needs. Consumer products firms producing toothpaste, shampoo, detergent, and so on might offer toll-free product information hotlines to address customer inquiries. Bicycle manufacturers might supply replacement parts for their products and repair damaged items. Discount stores might offer money-back guarantees for items that were not considered to be of high quality by purchasers.

Brokerage houses might send "thank you" letters to new customers in appreciation of their patronage. Hospitals and medical clinics might provide follow-up inquiries to check the status of patients who were recently treated. These follow-up activities greatly influence customer perceptions regarding the quality of delivered goods and services and are, therefore, critical to the success of any business entity.

Support Activities

Support activities consist of those pursuits that *indirectly* contribute to the production of specific goods and services. These are broad-based activities that influence all departments within organizations, regardless of role or function.

There are four support activities that are common to all organizations: firm infrastructure, human resource management, technology development, and procurement. These four support activities are identified as follows:

Firm Infrastructure

Firm infrastructure activities involve general administration pursuits (e.g., management, accounting). Instead of benefiting single departments or small groups of departments, these activities impact organizations in their entirety.

Human Resource Management

Human resource management activities involve all employment and employment-related pursuits of organizations including staffing, training, employee and labor relations, and compensation. These activities focus on the numerous workforce management issues and concerns that impact business entities.

Technology Development

Technology development activities involve all pursuits associated with the discovery and implementation of technologies that benefit organizations. Technology takes many forms, including know-how, product design, servicing procedures, and innovative equipment. These activities seek to incorporate innovations into business entities in order to reap associated benefits.

Procurement

Procurement activities involve all pursuits related to the acquisition of goods and services from outside vendors and suppliers. Examples include purchases of raw materials, machinery and equipment, office equipment and supplies (e.g., copiers, fax machines, computers, paper, pens), buildings, and so on. These acquisitions activities supply entities with the wealth of components necessary to pursue their missions.

In Practice

Each of the nine value activities identified by Porter represents an opportunity to create value. The more proficiently entities perform these value activities, the greater the value of their final products and resulting margins. A key strength of Porter's Value Chain is that it forces business entities to view the value creation process on an activity, rather than global, level. Value is the product of multiple activities performed by entities. High performance in one value activity can be neutralized by low performance in another. Entities must, therefore, work to ensure that each of the nine value activities is performed at optimal levels. By performing these activities better than competitors, business establishments create more value in the products they offer—a key source of competitive advantage.

In Summary

By identifying the nine value-producing activities that are common to all organizations, Porter's Value Chain provides useful insights into value and the value creation process. By understanding Porter's Value Chain, marketers and their organizations are better prepared to produce and provide goods and services that possess value—an essential task given the competitive nature of the marketplace.

REFERENCE:

Porter, Michael E. *Competitive Advantage: Creating and Sustaining Superior Performance.* New York: The Free Press, 1998.

Michael Porter's Generic Strategies

27

Characterized by intense competition and rivalry, the business environment poses extreme challenges for marketers seeking to successfully address the wants and needs of their target markets and ultimately achieve growth and prosperity. In addressing this turbulent environment, marketers must be armed with appropriate strategies that will allow them to outperform industry competitors. The process of formulating such strategies, however, is quite complex. Fortunately, marketers can turn to the work of Michael Porter for guidance in determining appropriate marketing strategies.

In an effort to assist marketers in determining appropriate strategies to pursue, Michael Porter developed a diagram which illustrates three strategies that can be employed to outperform industry competitors. Porter termed these alternatives "generic strategies" because of their applicability across industries. These strategies, which are illustrated in Figure 27-1, include overall cost leadership, differentiation, and focus. The particular strategy selected by entities depends on their strategic advantages and target markets. Porter's three generic strategies are defined as follows:

Overall Cost Leadership

The first strategy that organizations can employ to outperform industry competitors is termed overall cost leadership. This strategy, which entails targeting broad markets, is based on organizations achieving efficiencies of greater magnitude than those achieved by their competitors. These entities essentially incorporate every available cost saving feature into their operations to gain strategic advantages over their competitors. Such cost savings can be derived from building efficient facilities; incorporating cost-saving technologies; maintaining strict overhead expenditure controls; and minimizing expenditures in the areas of research and development, advertising, and so on. By achieving operational efficiencies that are greater than those of competitors, business entities can produce and provide goods and services at reduced costs, thus allowing them to garner above average returns in comparison to their competitors.

Differentiation

Another strategy that can be employed by organizations to outperform industry competitors is known as differentiation. This strategy, which involves targeting broad markets, is based on producing and providing

FIGURE 27-1: Porter's Generic Strategies

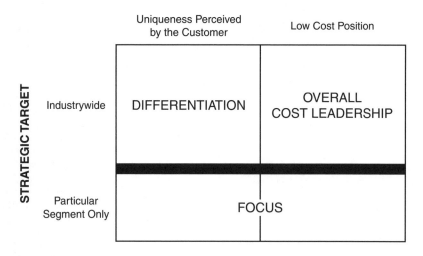

goods and services that are perceived by customers to be unique. Entities can differentiate their products through such methods as technology leadership, product design and functionality, product efficiency
and effectiveness, and customer service.

The exclusivity associated with these unique offerings grants entities a
degree of leverage over customers. After all, customers cannot purchase
these differentiated offerings from any other entity. This aspect also
reduces customer price sensitivity, allowing for enhanced pricing lati-
tude and greater possible returns.

Focus

A final strategy that organizations can employ to outperform industry
competitors is termed focus. Organizations using this strategy focus
exclusively on particular market segments in an effort to serve these
groups better than other entities. By concentrating on serving the wants
and needs of particular market segments, these entities can potentially
achieve success through cost leadership, differentiation, or both.

In Practice

Each of Porter's Generic Strategies can be used successfully by institutions. The particular strategy selected, however, is dependent on the
strategic advantages possessed by entities and the particular markets
sought.

Marketers ideally should assess the strategic capabilities of their organizations, determine the markets sought, and then select appropriate
strategies from Porter's framework. A computer manufacturer, for
example, that exclusively sells mainframe computers to government
entities would do well to adopt the focus strategy, whereas a firm offering broad-based technology products to a national audience would fair
better with a cost leadership or differentiation strategy.

Many smaller banks, restaurants, shipping firms, and similar entities are primarily segment-oriented, often limiting service delivery to

defined geographic markets and sometimes further segmenting these markets by addressing only certain wants and needs. These entities would do well to adopt the focus strategy, where they could potentially achieve success through cost leadership, differentiation, or both. Their larger counterparts which target broad markets, as Porter's framework illustrates, would best be served by the cost leadership or differentiation strategy. As these examples clearly indicate, the strategy selected is dependent on institutional capabilities and markets sought.

It should be noted that entities rarely achieve success through the use of multiple strategies. The pursuit of markets using multiple strategies places a significant burden on institutional resources, increasing the likelihood of decline and failure. It, therefore, is highly recommended that entities select only one of Porter's three generic strategies to pursue, thus avoiding potential resource allocation dilemmas.

In Summary

Through his identification and explanation of the three strategies that can be employed to outperform industry competitors, Michael Porter has provided a useful reference for marketers seeking guidance in formulating marketing strategy. With this information, marketers are better prepared to select appropriate strategies that will yield enduring marketing success.

REFERENCE:

Porter, Michael E. *Competitive Strategy: Techniques for Analyzing Industries and Competitors*. New York: The Free Press, 1998.

THE RIES & TROUT
MARKETING WARFARE STRATEGIES

28

Without question, business entities must attract and retain customers in order to survive and ultimately prosper. Success at attracting and retaining customers ultimately determines the share of the market—the market share—held by entities.

Market share is defined as an entity's portion, expressed as a percentage, of the total sales in a given market for a given product. The entity that possesses the greatest market share is known as the market leader—an enviable position to hold.

One of the most significant obstacles to gaining market share is that of competition. Business entities compete in an environment characterized by intense competition and rivalry. In their given markets, these organizations vie against one another for the valuable patronage of customers.

The term *competition* brings to mind images of contests, challenges, and so on and is a quite fitting descriptor for the business environment. However, two authors view the marketing process as so intensely competitive that it is deserving of a most intense analogy—war.

In their 1986 book entitled *Marketing Warfare*, Al Ries and Jack Trout contend that "marketing is war" and apply warfare strategies and tactics to the marketing process. Ries and Trout specifically note that being customer-oriented alone is not enough to achieve marketing success. Entities must also be competitor-oriented, directing attention to the identification of competitors and the analysis of their strengths and weaknesses in an effort to wage marketing war.

In order to be successful, marketing campaigns must be planned like military campaigns. Marketers must, therefore, understand warfare principles and be able to implement these strategies and tactics effectively. They, for example, must actively engage in the strategic planning process, seeking to formulate organizational goals and the action plans necessary for achieving these initiatives. They, too, must be skilled at anticipating competitive responses to various actions. Marketers must also be proficient at gaining marketplace intelligence in order to plan and launch successful attacks. Not only must operations be planned in a militaristic fashion, but the marketers involved in implementing these pursuits must possess characteristics often associated with military leaders—character, perseverance, discipline, loyalty, and the like.

According to Ries and Trout, marketing warfare can be waged using four different strategies: defensive warfare, offensive warfare, flanking warfare, and guerrilla warfare. As illustrated in Table 28-1, each strategy involves a number of basic, defining principles. The particular warfare strategy selected is dependent on the market position held by an entity. Accompanied by various industry examples, these four marketing warfare strategies are explained as follows:

Defensive Warfare

The defensive form of warfare should only be used by market leaders. Entities that possess such enviable positions should not, however, enter a hold-and-maintain mode. Instead, they should seek continuous improvement by attacking themselves. This involves the routine introduction of new and enhanced offerings that render existing products obsolete. Such offerings ultimately improve the already positive market positions held by market leaders.

It should be noted that when rivals orchestrate strong competitive moves, market leaders must take steps to block these actions, often by copying the particular competitor's move. By copying a competitor's move, a tit-for-tat philosophy, entities can maintain their market leadership positions by leveraging their market dominance. Blocking ensures that market leadership does not erode.

The leading banking institution in a community, for example, occupies the most powerful position in the minds of consumers. Obviously, the entity would like to maintain its leadership status. This, however, is not accomplished by complacency. Instead, the bank must actively seek to attack itself by enhancing existing services and adding new services.

TABLE 28-1: The Ries & Trout Marketing Warfare Strategies

Defensive Warfare

Principle 1: Only the market leader should consider playing defense.

Principle 2: The best defensive strategy is the courage to attack yourself.

Principle 3: Strong competitive moves should always be blocked.

Offensive Warfare

Principle 1: The main consideration is the strength of the leader's position.

Principle 2: Find a weakness in the leader's strength and attack at that point.

Principle 3: Launch the attack on as narrow a front as possible.

Flanking Warfare

Principle 1: A good flanking move must be made into an uncontested area.

Principle 2: Tactical surprise ought to be an important element of the plan.

Principle 3: The pursuit is just as critical as the attack itself.

Guerrilla Warfare

Principle 1: Find a segment of the market small enough to defend.

Principle 2: No matter how successful you become, never act like the leader.

Principle 3: Be prepared to bug out at a moment's notice.

Derived from information in *Marketing Warfare* by Al Ries and Jack Trout. New York: McGraw-Hill, 1986: 55-58, 68-72, 84-87, 101-107.

The bank might offer extended hours, better interest rates, more convenient locations, or any other feature that improves its existing service array. If the bank's market position is threatened by a rival, the entity must vigorously counter the threat by copying the competitor's move. If, for example, a rival bank seeks to increase its market share by opening on Saturdays, the market leader should block the move by opening on Saturdays as well. The leader's powerful market position gives it the upper hand, even if it follows the move of a competitor.

Offensive Warfare

Offensive warfare should be used by those entities falling just behind market leaders. These entities must target leaders, seeking to shift market share away from their powerful positions, preferably at points of weakness. Here, attacks should be initiated on very narrow fronts, perhaps on single products or small groups of offerings rather than entire product lines.

A fast food restaurant, for example, that finds itself trailing the market leader has a much more difficult task at hand than that of the leader. The trailing restaurant must, in essence, find ways to reduce the leader's market share, gathering the fallout to better its own market position. The restaurant would do well to study the leader and select a front to charge. Perhaps the restaurant could challenge the leader for its health-conscious customer population by introducing nutritious menu items. The leader, of course, could block the move, illustrating the difficult position of trailing entities in the battle for market share.

Flanking Warfare

The flanking warfare strategy is useful for any entity seeking to gain market share. This strategy involves the identification and occupation of new market segments. Although difficult to discover and develop, new segments offer open, uncontested terrain for flankers to occupy. The success of a flanking attack is largely related to the degree of surprise achieved. The element of surprise provides valuable time for flankers to establish beachheads within these new segments, making competitive responses much more difficult or even impossible. It is important to remember that after flanking attacks, marketers must diligently pursue the targeted market segments. All too often, entities fail to maintain the intensity of campaigns after initial marketing success. Attack and pursuit are of equally critical importance in the achievement of marketing success.

Newly discovered market segments offer growth opportunities for any business entity, regardless of its size or market position. The difficulty is in the discovery of these new segments. Increasing industrialization in a community might lead an automobile dealership, for example, to address the transportation needs associated with this development by upgrading its inventory to include heavy trucks. This new opportunity could be exploited for significant gains, resulting in control of the new segment. The more quickly the dealership targets and serves the new segment, the more likely its success as its rivals struggle to mount competitive responses. If success is achieved in the heavy truck segment, marketers must be sure to maintain the intensity demonstrated during the flanking attack to ensure the entity's enduring dominance in the new segment.

Guerrilla Warfare

Guerrilla warfare is most appropriately used by smaller entities competing in a market of larger competitors. These smaller entities do not possess the resources to compete directly with market leaders. Instead, they must identify small market segments where they can maintain leadership positions. Small entities must understand and appreciate their status and never be lulled by success into behaving like market leaders. These small entities must be quick in every regard, entering segments when they become desirable and exiting segments when they become undesirable.

A small hardware store in a community, for example, should think small by selecting a narrow segment within the larger market to serve. The store might possibly seek to be the preferred hardware supplier for individuals residing in a certain geographic area of the community.

Importantly, this small hardware store should respect its position in the broad market. Regardless of its success, the store must avoid acting like the market leader. It must emphasize rapidity which will enable it to capitalize on emerging opportunities.

In Summary

With their contention that "marketing is war," Ries and Trout provide a very useful, militaristic analogy for the marketing process. Their work is quite beneficial in that it introduces and advocates a competitor-orientation to marketing and provides an array of strategies that can be employed to increase market share.

Given the competitive nature of the business environment and the necessity for entities to attract and retain customers, marketers would do well to remember the useful guidelines offered by Ries and Trout. The authors have accurately identified successful strategies for waging marketing war.

REFERENCE:

Ries, Al, and Jack Trout. *Marketing Warfare*. New York: McGraw-Hill, 1986.

THE BLAKE & MOUTON SALES GRID

29

Personal selling is a promotional method involving the use of a sales force to convey messages. This promotional method is used extensively in the marketplace, most notably in the automobile, advertising, industrial equipment, pharmaceutical, and insurance industries. Personal selling, however, is also used in industries that are not traditionally associated with this promotional method, such as banking, where officers visit potential individual and institutional clients seeking to gain their patronage.

Sales representatives are often evaluated using some sort of quota, where performance is measured by comparing actual sales with prior-conceived sales goals for a given time period. This practice accurately assesses sales outcomes but does little to assess the techniques that sales representatives use in carrying out their assigned duties and responsibilities. The sales approaches used by representatives are certainly of great importance to entities. Sales agents do, after all, represent organizations. With the introduction of the Sales Grid, an evaluative tool developed by Robert Blake and Jane Mouton, the process of assessing the techniques used by sales representatives was greatly enhanced.

Illustrated in Figure 29-1, the Blake and Mouton Sales Grid consists of a nine-point horizontal scale that measures "concern for the sale" and a nine-point vertical scale that measures "concern for the customer." On these scales, 9 represents maximum concern and 1 represents minimum concern. A sales representative is evaluated first on his or her concern for the sale and then on his or her concern for the customer. This evaluation yields a two-number score that describes the sales representative's approach to selling. Of the 81 possible "concern for the sale" and "concern for the customer" combinations on the Sales Grid, Blake and Mouton specifically identify and describe five which are explained as follows:

Location 9,1
(Push-the-Product Orientation)

The 9,1 strategy, located in the lower right corner of the Sales Grid, involves a complete concern for making the sale with little or no regard for the customer. Due to its total focus on making the sale, this strategy is termed the Push-the-Product Orientation. Sales agents with such orientations use hard sell, pressure-oriented tactics to generate sales. Their concern for the sale is so pronounced that it is to the detriment of customers. Quite obviously, customers resent this approach. Here, there is virtually no concern for the needs, preferences, or feelings of customers.

Location 1,9
(People Orientation)

The 1,9 strategy, located in the upper left corner of the Sales Grid, involves little or no concern for the sale and maximum concern for the customer and is thus termed the People Orientation. Sales representatives who practice this strategy seek to develop bonds with customers in hopes that sales will be generated through these relationships. Very little direct persuasion is used in their sales pitches. To the detriment of themselves and their organizations, salespersons become dependent on friendships, rather than effective sales techniques, for success.

Location 1,1
(Take-It-or-Leave-It Orientation)

The 1,1 strategy, located in the Sales Grid's lower left corner, is termed the Take-It-or-Leave-It Orientation. This approach involves little or no concern for both the sale and the customer. These sales representatives operate in a passive manner, doing nothing to develop customer relationships or communicate product features and benefits. Products are simply placed before customers who decide whether or not to purchase the offerings without any assistance or influence from sales agents. With complete disregard for both sales and customers, these sales representatives serve to the detriment of all parties involved: themselves, their organizations, and their customers.

FIGURE 29-1: The Blake & Mouton Sales Grid

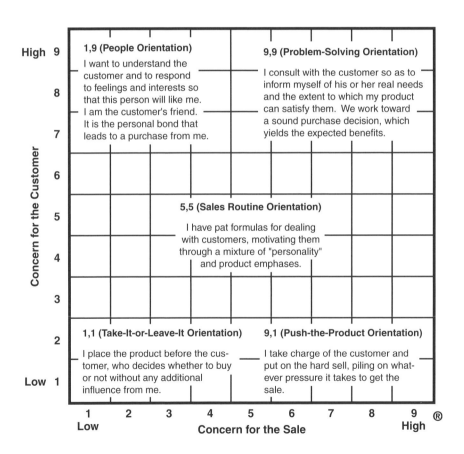

Location 5,5
(Sales Routine Orientation)

The 5,5 strategy, located in the center of the Sales Grid, represents a middle-of-the-road approach. Termed the Sales Routine Orientation, this approach involves a moderate amount of concern for both the sale and the customer. Here, sales representatives seek to make customers comfortable through light conversation and "small talk" as they

FIGURE 29-2: A Sales Force Assessment Using the Sales Grid

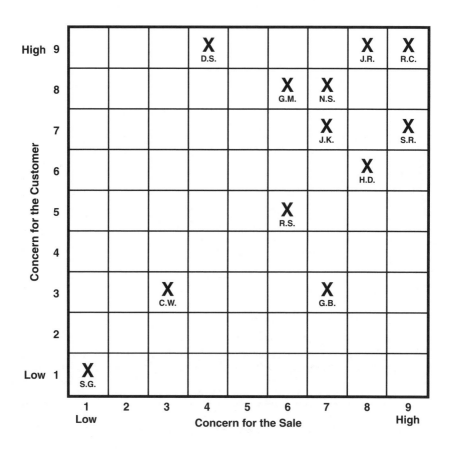

present their pat formulas for generating sales. Their pat formulas are well-rehearsed sales presentations that come across rather mechanically. Although their performance is not stellar, sales representatives using this approach do achieve adequate results.

Location 9,9
(Problem-Solving Orientation)

The 9,9 strategy, located in the Sales Grid's upper right corner, is termed the Problem-Solving Orientation. This approach involves maximum concern for both the sale and the customer. Sales representatives using this strategy possess a highly detailed knowledge of both the products they sell and the specific needs of their customers. Here, sales agents work closely with customers to assist them in making sound purchase decisions that meet and exceed expectations, yielding desired benefits.

These sales representatives provide solutions for customers. Given its maximum concern for both the sale and the customer, the 9,9 strategy yields superior results. Sales representatives practicing this strategy are assets to both their organizations and the customers they serve. Clearly, the 9,9 strategy is the most desirable sales approach.

In Practice

Business entities can greatly benefit by using the Blake and Mouton Sales Grid to assess the techniques used by their sales representatives. By evaluating these techniques, entities can identify strengths and weaknesses within their sales operations, taking corrective actions when necessary to ensure optimal performance.

Figure 29-2 illustrates the usefulness of the Sales Grid. Here, an entity has evaluated each of its twelve sales representatives and plotted the resulting scores on the Sales Grid using an "X" accompanied by each sales agent's initials. This Grid reveals that the entity's sales force primarily uses sales techniques that are pitched toward the 9,9 Problem-Solving Orientation. Notably, it also identifies a few sales agents whose techniques warrant alteration.

The Sales Grid is useful not only as an assessment tool, but also as a training tool for new sales representatives. By instilling the 9,9 approach in sales trainees, these new recruits will be fully aware of the importance of carrying out their duties and responsibilities in a problem-solving fashion. The Sales Grid can also be employed as a self-assessment tool for sales representatives. When used in this manner, sales representatives are reminded of desirable and undesirable approaches to selling and can alter their techniques accordingly.

Although the Sales Grid is primarily designed as a tool for the evaluation of sales representatives, it can productively be used to assess any occupation that involves customer contact. Whenever employees come into contact with customers, they become sales representatives for their organizations and the Sales Grid applies. When viewed in this manner, the Sales Grid becomes a helpful tool for evaluating the customer service techniques of virtually any type of employee—executives, managers, secretaries, custodians, and so on.

In Summary

The Blake and Mouton Sales Grid provides a highly useful tool for evaluating the techniques used by sales representatives in carrying out their duties and responsibilities. It can also effectively assess the approaches of all other employees who come into contact with customers. By using the Sales Grid, business entities can ensure that all employees charged with interacting with customers are performing at optimal levels.

REFERENCE:

Blake, Robert R., and Jane Srygley Mouton. *The Grid for Sales Excellence: New Insights into a Proven System of Effective Sales.* 2d ed. New York: McGraw-Hill, 1980.

Philip Kotler's
Marketing Plan

30

Given the scope and diversity of marketing activities, it is essential for marketers to formalize their pursuits on at least an annual basis through the development of comprehensive marketing plans. By reducing marketing pursuits to writing, marketers are forced to think through upcoming periods, perform routine marketing analyses, and set marketing goals and objectives that are properly aligned with institutional goals and objectives.

Once completed, marketing plans act as road maps, allowing marketers to assess their progress over time, making adjustments as necessary. Without formal marketing plans, marketers will likely find themselves managing marketing pursuits in a reactive fashion, lacking insight, direction, and control—a formula for disaster.

Developing marketing plans requires significant effort and attention. Among other things, these plans require accurate product, market, and competitor information, as well as insightful and creative thinking on the part of plan authors and contributors. Marketing plans also must be well written and presented in an orderly fashion—aspects that greatly enhance the usefulness of these documents.

Although there are no mandatory guidelines for the format of marketing plans, a quite useful outline for such a plan has been offered by Philip Kotler. Illustrated in Figure 30-1, Kotler's Marketing Plan consists of eight sections, namely an executive summary and table of contents, an overview of the current marketing situation, an opportunity and issue analysis, the identification of marketing objectives, the identification of the marketing strategy to be employed, the identification of action programs for attaining strategic objectives, a projected profit-and-loss statement, and the identification of controls for monitoring plan performance.

Section I: Executive Summary & Table of Contents

Kotler's Marketing Plan begins with an executive summary and table of contents. The executive summary specifically provides a concise overview of plan contents, emphasizing main goals and recommendations. This summary allows readers to quickly review the major facets of the marketing plan that follows. The executive summary is followed by a table of contents which outlines the given marketing plan and provides a page numbering system to assist readers in locating major plan components. Although this section is listed first, it is by necessity, of course, developed last.

Section II: Current Marketing Situation

The executive summary and table of contents section is followed by a review of the current marketing situation. Here, an overview of current marketing pursuits is presented, providing background information as necessary. This section includes information and analyses regarding customers, markets, and competitors, along with relevant performance data including sales, cost, and profit information. This section provides readers with a comprehensive snapshot of current marketing efforts.

Section III: Opportunity & Issue Analysis

After identifying the current marketing situation, an opportunity and issue analysis is presented. In this section, the strengths, weaknesses, opportunities, and threats associated with product offerings are identified. Methods for capitalizing on the identified strengths and opportunities are noted, as are methods for avoiding or eliminating weaknesses and threats.

After SWOT information has been presented and addressed, relevant issues and concerns are identified. Such issues and concerns might include whether particular markets should be pursued; whether promotional expenditures should be increased or decreased; whether given products should continue to be offered, be discontinued, or be modified; and so on.

Section IV: Objectives

Once opportunities and issues have been identified and addressed, broad marketing objectives for the upcoming period are presented. A fast food restaurant might, for example, seek to increase its customer traffic by 10% over the next six months. A shipping company might seek to increase its deliveries by 25% over the next two years. A computer manufacturer might wish to increase sales by $15 million over

FIGURE 30-1: Components of Kotler's Marketing Plan

I	Executive Summary & Table of Contents
II	Current Marketing Situation
III	Opportunity & Issue Analysis
IV	Objectives
V	Marketing Strategy
VI	Action Programs
VII	Projected Profit-&-Loss Statement
VIII	Controls

Adapted from MARKETING MANAGEMENT: THE MILLENNIUM EDITION 10/E by Kotler, Philip. © 2000. Reprinted by permission of Pearson Education, Inc., Upper Saddle River, NJ.

the next year. Depending on the particular organization, the number of identified objectives may be as few as one or quite numerous.

Section V: Marketing Strategy

The objectives section of the marketing plan is followed by the identification of broad marketing strategies that will be used to achieve identified objectives. This section essentially presents the broad marketing "game plan." The fast food restaurant seeking to increase customer traffic might designate a strategy of increasing public awareness of its product offerings, hours of operation, and courteous staff. The shipping company seeking to increase deliveries might devise a strategy of targeting small businesses in an effort to acquire their valuable patronage.

The computer manufacturer seeking to increase sales might formulate a strategy that involves increasing consumer awareness of its products, increasing the size of its sales force, and improving its product presence at retail establishments. These broad strategies are operationalized through the implementation of action programs identified in the following section.

Section VI: Action Programs

The marketing strategy section of the marketing plan is followed by the identification of action programs that specify how organizations plan to accomplish their broad marketing goals. The fast food restaurant would list how it plans to increase consumer awareness, possibly through the development of a new ad campaign. It would also identify the nature of the campaign, the ad media to be used, the frequency of ad placement, and related data. The shipping company would identify the particular businesses to be targeted by its campaign, the nature of the message to be conveyed, and the timeline for implementation.

The computer manufacturer would discuss its specific plans for increasing sales, providing detailed information related to a possible new ad campaign, the hiring and training of new sales agents, and methods for improving its product presence at retail establishments. Action programs are very specific and itemize the tactical operations necessary to carry out identified marketing strategies.

Section VII: Projected Profit-&-Loss Statement

After action programs have been identified, a projected profit-and-loss statement is presented, where expected financial outcomes are identified, along with a supporting budget. The revenue side of the projected profit-and-loss statement presents anticipated cash inflows resulting from marketing efforts, while the expense side lists associated marketing costs (e.g., costs associated with advertising and distribution). The difference between the revenue side and the expense side reflects projected profit.

Section VIII: Controls

The final section of the marketing plan identifies mechanisms for monitoring the progress of marketing pursuits. Importantly, this section includes a timeline for implementing associated marketing activities and for reviewing the results of those activities. (Marketers should formally monitor marketing progress on either a monthly or a quarterly basis.) This section also includes contingency plans for use in the event that undesirable results occur.

In Summary

The complex and varied array of marketing activities within organizations necessitates the development and assembly of formal marketing plans. These plans force marketers to think through upcoming periods, perform routine marketing analyses, and set appropriate marketing goals and objectives. When completed, marketing plans serve as road maps that guide marketers, allowing them to proactively, rather than reactively, address and manage marketing pursuits.

Given the critical importance of marketing plans, marketers must take great care in preparation of these documents. Kotler's Marketing

Plan provides marketers with a useful framework for presenting such a plan in an orderly fashion. By using Kotler's framework, marketers are assured that their marketing plans contain necessary plan components and that these elements are presented appropriately. When content is added to this framework, marketers gain an invaluable marketing resource.

REFERENCE:

Kotler, Philip. *Marketing Management: The Millennium Edition.* 10th ed. Upper Saddle River, NJ: Prentice Hall, 2000.

APPENDIX

AN INTRODUCTION
TO MARKETING

An Introduction
to Marketing

Modern organizations compete in what might be considered the most competitive marketplace of all time in an environment of immense and ever-increasing complexity. On an ongoing basis, establishments of all kinds—banks, airlines, automobile manufacturers, technology firms, hospitals, hotels, restaurants, and so on—vie against one another in their respective markets for the opportunity to serve customers. Each of these organizations ultimately is in search of growth and prosperity, and the best managed of these entities will indeed realize this goal.

Marketing is possibly the most critical management responsibility associated with the pursuit and realization of growth and prosperity. Marketing can broadly be defined as *a management process that involves the assessment of customer wants and needs, and the performance of all activities associated with the development, pricing, provision, and promotion of product solutions that satisfy those wants and needs.*

Although most often associated with advertising and sales, marketing is much more encompassing as its definition implies. Aside from promotions activities, marketing includes such critical functions as environmental scanning, wants and needs assessment, new product development, target marketing, product pricing, product distribution, and market research.

Wants & Needs

Marketing pursuits normally begin with assessing the wants and needs of customers. The terms *want* and *need* are often used interchangeably in society; however, these words are actually quite distinct, particularly when associated with marketing goods and services. A *need* is something that a person requires for well-being and possibly survival, while a *want* is something that a person simply desires.

Items like food, water, electricity for the home, and gasoline for auto-mobile transportation to work are purchased and consumed out of necessity and, therefore, represent needs. Vacation getaways, luxury automobiles, expensive jewelry, and elaborate home entertainment systems, however, represent wants in that the products are not necessities.

Products: Goods & Services

The marketplace is filled with countless wants and needs with hand-some rewards being offered to organizations that can satisfy these wants and needs with product solutions. The term *product* refers to any offering provided by an entity for purchase and consumption. A product can be a good (a tangible item), a service (an intangible item), or a hybrid (an item with tangible and intangible characteristics). This array of product variants can be illustrated on a continuum with pure goods (tangible items) at one end and pure services (intangible items) at the other end. Figure A-1 illustrates this continuum along with several example products that have been placed on the continuum based on their tangibility or lack thereof.

Pure goods, like jewelry, furniture, television sets, and automobiles, can be viewed in reasonable isolation from any service component, while pure services, like haircuts, banking transactions, physical examina-tions, shipping services, and air carrier transportation, can be isolated from any tangible offering.

Food ordered at a restaurant, however, represents a hybrid product in that a service (waitstaff assistance and food preparation) must accom-pany the good that is provided (the particular meal that was ordered). Prescription contact lenses would also represent a hybrid product in that a service (diagnosis by a medical professional) must accompany the delivery of the good that is provided (the particular contact lenses).

Beyond goods and services, it is important to note that ideas and philosophies can also be considered products—intangible, of course. Political candidates campaigning for public office and cause-related organizations seeking to encourage particular actions (e.g., charitable donations, healthy lifestyles), are, in essence, attempting to sell products to designated populations.

Regardless of their tangibility or lack thereof, products that ineffectively address the wants and needs of customers will surely fail. By appropriately addressing customer wants and needs, marketers increase the likelihood that their goods and services will achieve commercial success.

Target Marketing

When organizations develop new products, marketers must determine which customer groups they wish to pursue and how they wish to present their products to these groups—a practice known as target marketing. Through target marketing, marketers customize product offerings and associated marketing activities in an effort to address the diverse wants and needs of specific customer groups.

Target marketing involves three interrelated activities: market segmentation, targeting, and product positioning. Market segmentation is the process of dividing a market into groups (segments) of individuals who share common characteristics. Once the market has been segmented, marketers engage in targeting where they select (target) attractive segments and focus their efforts on satisfying the wants and needs of these groups. These targeted segments are known as an entity's target market. Product positioning follows targeting and involves the determination

FIGURE A-1: The Product Continuum

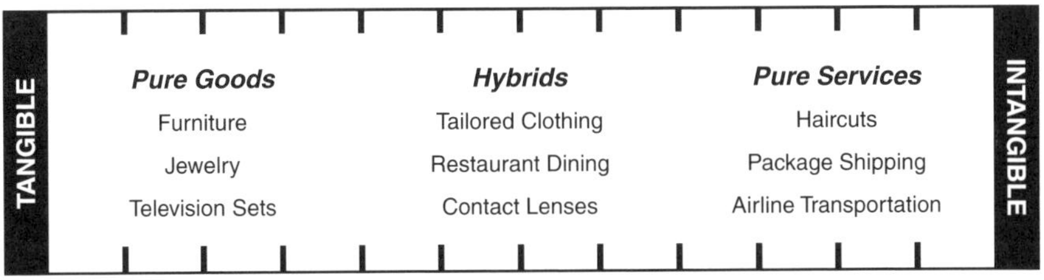

TANGIBLE	Pure Goods	Hybrids	Pure Services	INTANGIBLE
	Furniture	Tailored Clothing	Haircuts	
	Jewelry	Restaurant Dining	Package Shipping	
	Television Sets	Contact Lenses	Airline Transportation	

of an appropriate and effective "image" for products to convey to customers. Here, marketers seek to influence customer perceptions related to particular goods and services.

Usefully, target marketing allows marketers to craft customized promotions campaigns designed to appeal to given segments. This customization increases the likelihood that targeted audiences will respond favorably to product offerings. Target marketing also allows marketers to make better use of their promotions resources in that marketing efforts can be directed toward specific audiences rather than entire markets.

The Marketing Mix

Upon identification of the particular segment or segments to pursue, marketers formulate the marketing mix for each customer group that is sought. Illustrated in Figure A-2, the marketing mix includes four interdependent components: product, price, place, and promotion. It is often referred to as the Four Ps of Marketing for obvious reasons. For each product offering, marketers must design each component of the marketing mix in a manner that will entice targeted customers. The components of the marketing mix are explained as follows:

Product

The product component of the marketing mix involves the development of goods and services that will meet and, ideally, exceed the wants and needs of targeted markets. For goods, product development involves, among other things, the actual physical assembly of the offerings. For services, product development involves the assembly of all components required for the services to be offered, such as office space, equipment, operating permits, and personnel.

Marketers must take great care in assembling product attributes for targeted customer segments. An appropriate "fit" between given product offerings and the wants and needs of targeted audiences is an essential requirement for marketing success.

FIGURE A-2: The Marketing Mix

Price

Price refers to the amount of money that must be paid by customers in order to acquire particular goods and services. The more features embedded in products, the greater they cost organizations to produce and provide. These costs, of course, are ultimately passed on to customers in the form of higher prices.

Plush retail outlets located in the community's highest traffic areas, the latest product technologies, elaborate and extensive product arrays, exceptional customer service, and so on all add to the costs associated with providing goods and services. Some consumers have the means and the desire for enhanced product offerings, while others do not.

There are, of course, limits to what individuals can and will pay for goods and services. Broadly speaking, a balance must be struck between the attributes of particular products and the prices charged for the offerings. This balance must meet the financial requirements of business entities and the financial means of prospective customers—items that must be thoroughly addressed prior to bringing products to market.

Place

The place component of the marketing mix, which is sometimes termed distribution, refers to all elements involved in making products available to customers. These activities include such tasks as the identification of distribution channels, the determination of inventory levels, and the management of warehousing issues. Other place activities include the determination of locations of availability and hours of operation.

Different products often require different place considerations. Automobile manufacturers would be concerned with creating and maintaining complex distribution linkages extending into and from their manufacturing plants to the various dealerships that sell their automobiles to customers. Food processing companies would be concerned with establishing an array of distribution linkages ultimately resulting in their food items garnering both shelf space in grocery stores and use in restaurants.

Banking institutions would be concerned with such place matters as the physical location and hours of operation of their establishments. Shipping firms would focus heavily on their geographic delivery areas. Air carriers would be concerned with traveler time/date/location preferences for departures and arrivals, aircraft placement plans, and linkages with airports.

Consumption cannot occur if products are not accessible to target markets, with ease of access positively influencing consumption. The place component of the marketing mix focuses on hastening the purchase process by making goods and services readily available to customers.

Promotion

The promotions component of the marketing mix involves all activities associated with communicating product attributes to target markets. Advertising is perhaps the best known promotional method; however, other forms exist including personal selling, sales promotion, public relations, and direct marketing. These five promotional methods combine to form what is referred to as the promotions, or communications, mix.

Business entities normally promote themselves using a variety of methods in their quest to entice customers to purchase and consume products. These techniques build product awareness by engaging potential customers and encouraging their patronage through the conveyance of product attributes.

Ongoing Marketing Surveillance

Throughout the marketing process, marketers must maintain a keen awareness of the environment by engaging in ongoing marketing surveillance. Marketing surveillance activities include assessing customer wants and needs, assessing the potential of markets, identifying market trends, monitoring product performance in given markets, monitoring the activities of competitors, and determining future marketing pursuits. Importantly, marketers must ensure that surveillance activities are sustained over time—an absolute necessity given the ever-changing nature of the marketplace.

In Summary

Marketing is possibly the most critical management responsibility associated with the pursuit and realization of growth and prosperity. The essential role of marketing is even more pronounced in the intensely competitive business environment where entities vie against one another in their respective markets for the opportunity to serve customers.

Given the importance of marketing, business entities must ensure that they devote sufficient resources to marketing and its many activities. The success of an organization is directly linked to its success in marketing.

Glossary

ADVERTISING   A promotional method involving the paid use of mass media to deliver messages. Examples include newspaper ads, magazine ads, television ads, radio ads, and billboards.

BRAND   A name, logo, slogan, or other reference that identifies goods and services, thus allowing consumers to differentiate product offerings.

BRAND EQUITY   The value of a brand.

BRAND PORTFOLIO   The overall collection of brands held by an organization.

COMMUNICATIONS MIX   The five promotional methods used by marketers to reach target markets: advertising, personal selling, sales promotion, public relations, and direct marketing. Also referred to as the promotions mix.

COMPETITIVE ADVANTAGE   Anything possessed by an organization that gives it an edge over its competitors.

COST   The amount of money that entities must spend to produce and/or provide goods and services.

DIRECT MARKETING   A promotional method involving the delivery of messages directly to consumers. Examples include direct-mail marketing, telemarketing, and catalog marketing.

DISTRIBUTION   All elements involved with making products available to target markets. Examples include the transportation of goods to retail establishments, the warehousing of finished products, and the determination of hours of operation. Sometimes used as an alternate term for the "place" aspect of the marketing mix.

ENVIRONMENTAL SCANNING   An externally-focused activity where marketers seek to assess the environment in an effort to identify marketplace trends.

FOUR Ps OF MARKETING   The four interdependent components of product, price, place, and promotion that must be formulated for each product offering in an effort to attract target markets. Also known as the marketing mix.

GOODS   Tangible product offerings.

MARGIN   The difference between the cost of producing and/or providing a product and the price received for the given offering.

MARKET   A broad collection of potential customers.

MARKET SEGMENT   A group of individuals within a market who share common characteristics (e.g., age, income, tastes, preferences).

MARKET SEGMENTATION   The process of dividing a market into groups (segments) of individuals who share common characteristics. Market segmentation is the first step of target marketing.

MARKET SHARE   An entity's portion, expressed as a percentage, of the total sales in a given market for a given product.

MARKETING   A management process that involves the assessment of customer wants and needs, and the performance of all activities associated with the development, pricing, provision, and promotion of product solutions that satisfy those wants and needs.

MARKETING MIX   The four interdependent components of product, price, place, and promotion that must be formulated for each product offering in an effort to attract target markets. Also known as the Four Ps of Marketing.

MARKETING PLAN   A formal document that describes and assesses the current marketing performance of an organization and sets marketing goals and objectives for the upcoming period.

NEEDS   Things that are required by individuals for well-being and possibly survival; necessities as opposed to desires.

NEW-TO-THE-WORLD PRODUCTS   Newly introduced products that define entirely new product categories never before offered to the public.

PERSONAL SELLING   A promotional method involving the use of a sales force to convey messages.

PLACE   One of the Four Ps of Marketing which involves the formulation of all elements associated with making products available to target markets. Examples include the transportation of goods to retail establishments, the warehousing of finished products, and the determination of hours of operation. Sometimes referred to as distribution.

PORTFOLIO ANALYSIS   An activity involving the comprehensive review and assessment of an organization's product offerings.

PRICE   (1) The amount of money that must be paid by customers in order to acquire particular goods and services. (2) One of the Four Ps of Marketing which involves the determination of a product's price and related pricing strategies in an effort to attract target markets.

PRODUCT   (1) Any offering provided by an entity for purchase and consumption. A product can be a good (a tangible item), a service (an intangible item), or a hybrid (an item with tangible and intangible characteristics). (2) One of the Four Ps of Marketing which involves the development of goods and services that will meet and, ideally, exceed the wants and needs of target markets.

PRODUCT DIFFERENTIATION   (1) The ability to distinguish a product from competitive offerings. (2) The development of distinguishable product features that allow offerings to easily be recognized by customers.

PRODUCT LIFE CYCLE   A model that illustrates the four stages of a product's development: introduction, growth, maturity, and decline.

PRODUCT PORTFOLIO   The overall collection of products offered by an entity.

PRODUCT POSITIONING   The process of determining an appropriate and effective "image" for products to convey to customers in an effort to influence their perceptions of goods and services. Product positioning is the final step of target marketing.

PROMOTION   (1) All activities associated with communicating a product's attributes to target markets. (2) One of the Four Ps of Marketing which involves the formulation of communications strategies and tactics that will effectively convey product attributes to target markets.

PROMOTIONS MIX   The five promotional methods used by marketers to reach target markets: advertising, personal selling, sales promotion, public relations, and direct marketing. Also referred to as the communications mix.

PUBLIC RELATIONS   A promotional method involving the use of publicity and other unpaid forms of promotion to deliver messages. Examples include press releases, open houses, facility tours, and educational seminars.

SALES PROMOTION   A promotional method involving the use of incentives to stimulate customer interest. Examples include discount coupons, free gifts, samples, and contests.

SERVICES   Intangible product offerings.

TARGET MARKET   The name given to a market segment that has been selected (targeted) by an organization.

TARGET MARKETING   A three-step process that involves the division of a market into segments (market segmentation), the selection of attractive segments to pursue (targeting), and the determination of an appropriate and effective "image" for products to convey to customers (product positioning).

TARGETING   The selection of attractive market segments to pursue. Targeting is the second step of target marketing.

WANTS   Things that are desired by individuals, but are not required for well-being and survival; desires as opposed to necessities.

References

Ansoff, H. Igor. *Corporate Strategy: An Analytic Approach to Business Policy for Growth and Expansion.* New York: McGraw-Hill, 1965.

Ansoff, H. Igor. *The New Corporate Strategy.* Rev. ed. New York: Wiley, 1988.

Berkowitz, Eric N., Roger A. Kerin, Steven W. Hartley, and William Rudelius. *Marketing.* 6th ed. New York: McGraw-Hill, 2000.

Berry, Leonard L. *Discovering the Soul of Service: The Nine Drivers of Sustainable Business Success.* New York: The Free Press, 1999.

Berthon, Pierre, James M. Hulbert, and Leyland F. Pitt. "Brand Management Prognostications." *MIT Sloan Management Review* 40, no. 2 (Winter 1999): 53-65.

Blake, Robert R., and Jane Srygley Mouton. *The Grid for Sales Excellence: New Insights into a Proven System of Effective Sales.* 2d ed. New York: McGraw-Hill, 1980.

Booz, Allen, & Hamilton. *Management of New Products.* New York: Booz, Allen, & Hamilton, 1968.

Booz, Allen, & Hamilton. *New Products Management for the 1980s.* New York: Booz, Allen, & Hamilton, 1982.

Calder, Bobby J., and Steven J. Reagan. "Brand Design." In *Kellogg on Marketing*, edited by Dawn Iacobucci. New York: Wiley, 2001.

Day, George S. *The Market Driven Organization: Understanding, Attracting, and Keeping Valuable Customers.* New York: The Free Press, 1999.

Dutka, Solomon. *DAGMAR: Defining Advertising Goals for Measured Advertising Results.* 2d ed. (1st ed. by Russell Colley). Lincolnwood, IL: NTC Business Books, 1995.

Henderson, Bruce D. "The Product Portfolio" (1970). In *Perspectives on Strategy from the Boston Consulting Group*, edited by Carl W. Stern and George Stalk, Jr. New York: Wiley, 1998.

Jain, Dipak. "Managing New Product Development for Strategic Competitive Advantage." In *Kellogg on Marketing*, edited by Dawn Iacobucci. New York: Wiley, 2001.

Keller, Kevin Lane. "The Brand Report Card." *Harvard Business Review* (January-February) 2000: 147-157.

Kotler, Philip. *Marketing Management: The Millennium Edition*. 10th ed. Upper Saddle River, NJ: Prentice Hall, 2000.

Kotler, Philip, and Gary Armstrong. *Principles of Marketing*. 8th ed. Upper Saddle River, NJ: Prentice Hall, 1999.

Lederer, Chris, and Sam Hill. "See Your Brands Through Your Customers' Eyes." *Harvard Business Review* (June) 2001: 125-133.

Lehmann, Donald R., and Russell S. Winer. *Analysis for Marketing Planning*. 5th ed. New York: McGraw-Hill, 2002.

Levitt, Theodore. "Marketing Myopia." *Harvard Business Review* (July-August) 1960: 45-56.

Levitt, Theodore. "Exploit the Product Life Cycle." *Harvard Business Review* (November-December) 1965: 81-94.

Levitt, Theodore. "Marketing Success Through Differentiation—of Anything." *Harvard Business Review* (January-February) 1980: 83-91.

Levitt, Theodore. *The Marketing Imagination*. New, expanded ed. New York: The Free Press, 1986.

Maslow, Abraham H. *The Maslow Business Reader*, edited by Deborah C. Stephens. New York: Wiley, 2000.

Mintzberg, Henry, and Ludo Van der Heyden. "Organigraphs: Drawing How Companies Really Work." *Harvard Business Review* (September-October) 1999: 87-94.

Osgood, Charles E., George J. Suci, and Percy H. Tannenbaum. *The Measurement of Meaning*. Urbana, IL: University of Illinois Press, 1957.

Porter, Michael E. *Competitive Advantage: Creating and Sustaining Superior Performance*. New York: The Free Press, 1998.

Porter, Michael E. *Competitive Strategy: Techniques for Analyzing Industries and Competitors*. New York: The Free Press, 1998.

Raphel, Murray, and Neil Raphel. *Up the Loyalty Ladder: Turning Sometime Customers into Full-Time Advocates of Your Business*. New York: HarperBusiness, 1995.

Ries, Al, and Jack Trout. *Marketing Warfare*. New York: McGraw-Hill, 1986.

Ries, Al, and Jack Trout. *Positioning: The Battle for Your Mind*. 20th anniversary ed. New York: McGraw-Hill, 2001.

Rogers, Everett M. *Diffusion of Innovations*. 4th ed. New York: The Free Press, 1995.

ABOUT THE AUTHOR

John L. Fortenberry, Jr. is founder and President of Oxford Crest, a management and marketing education firm based in Oxford, Mississippi. Dr. Fortenberry founded Oxford Crest to provide management and marketing guidance to executives, scholars, and students through educational events and informative publications.

In addition to his duties at Oxford Crest, Dr. Fortenberry serves as the James K. Elrod Professor of Health Care Administration at Louisiana State University in Shreveport.

Dr. Fortenberry received his BBA from the University of Mississippi, his MBA from Mississippi College, and his Ph.D. from Auburn University.